Fundamentals of Copy & Layout

Albert C. Book
C. Dennis Schick

NTC Business Books
a division of National Textbook Company • Lincolnwood Illinois U.S.A.

Published by NTC Business Books, an imprint of
National Textbook Company, 4255 West Touhy Avenue,
Lincolnwood (Chicago), Illinois 60646-1975. Copyright
©1984 by Albert C. Book and C. Dennis Schick. All rights
reserved. No part of this book may be reproduced, stored
in a retrieval system, or transmitted in any form, or by
any means, electronic, mechanical, photocopying or
otherwise, without the prior written permission of
National Textbook Company.
Library of Congress Catalog Card No. LC82-71763.
Manufactured in the United States of America.

5 6 7 8 9 0 ML 0 9 8 7 6 5 4 3 2 1

Contents

Introduction

The American novelist Henry James once wrote, "There is no work of literary or any other art that any human being is under the smallest obligation to like."

While the advertising practitioner does not have to make his audience "like" his efforts, he does have to stimulate people to go out and buy his product. This is no easy task. It takes a combination of skills, as well as that elusive element called creativity.

Creativity might be termed originality of thought and expression. It is the innovative kind of thinking that makes advertising copy and design interesting and exciting. Indispensable though it is, however, creativity cannot be reduced to a set of rules or even guidelines. For that reason, it would be wrong to assume that an instructor—or a book—could teach it. That would be akin to assuming that inspiration can be taught. It simply can't be done.

The Fundamentals of Copy and Layout does not deal in such assumptions. It attempts, primarily, to convey basic information without which even the most creative person attempting to practice advertising would be handicapped.

Of course, beyond a knowledge of the basics, there are other attributes the aspiring advertising practitioner should possess. For instance, he or she should be curious, open-minded, and tirelessly motivated. He or she should have a broad vocabulary, in order to use words thoughtfully and skillfully. With this advantage, the advertising professional has a better chance of establishing rapport with the audience. But in order to go one step further—to convince—he must be more than clever. He must bring to his craft a knowledge of literature, politics, popular culture, technology, geography, history and psychology. He should even know jargon—the better to avoid it.

The true advertising professional must obviously learn all about the product or service in order to present its benefits and virtues in a clear, honest, and distinctive manner. He must learn to use research as an ally.

He must learn to write with clarity, lucidity, style, precision, imagination, and even a smidgen of controlled passion.

He must, above all, adhere to a personal and professional code of ethics.

An attempt to cover all these areas comprehensively in a manual would be an impossible task. *The Fundamentals of Copy and Layout*, therefore, should be regarded as a beginning. It is designed for people who are starting their advertising education or career. However, it might also prove useful to advanced students and practitioners who need to be reminded (as everyone does occasionally) of the basic principles of their profession.

PART I
Creative Philosophies

Creative Philosophies

There are probably as many theories about how advertising works—and how the creative aspects of advertising work—as there are advertising practitioners. And since many outsiders claim to be experts and freely give advice about the advertising business, there are undoubtedly more advertising philosophies than there are people actually engaged in the profession of advertising.

On the other hand, although most advertising people can tell you about their advertising successes (and failures), many are unable to explain why their ad campaigns succeeded (or failed). By implication, a creative philosophy should suggest both how the creative process operates in general and why it works or doesn't work in specific instances.

A number of highly successful advertising people have formulated such theories, and they are worth listening to. Some of them have shared their thoughts through agency house ads. Others have done so in articles and books. A close examination of their creative philosophies, born out of experience, intuition, and many successful campaigns, can be extremely valuable in providing insights into the whole area of creativity in advertising.

FAIRFAX M. CONE
Foote, Cone & Belding

Fairfax Cone's creative philosophy is based on his definition of advertising: something you do when you cannot send a salesperson. According to Cone, advertising must achieve what a good salesperson achieves—that is, sales. And it must reflect the qualities a good salesperson possesses.

I believe that every honest advertisement will be successful that meets the requirements of only five rules . . . and that no advertising can succeed that fails to meet any one of them; they are not divisible. . . .

The first rule for good advertising is that it must immediately make clear what the basic proposition is. Few if any people have either the time or the inclination to try to solve the puzzle of obscure advertising promises.

Second, it is equally important to successful advertising that what is clear shall also be important. The proposition must express a well-defined value.

Third, the successful advertisement will express the value of the offering in personal terms. It will be beamed directly at the most logical prospects for the proposition; no one else matters.

Source: Fairfax M. Cone, *With All Its Faults* (Boston: Little, Brown, 1969), pp. 58–60.

Fourth, good advertising will always express the personality of the advertiser, for a promise is only as good as its maker.

Finally, a successful advertisement will always demand action. It will ask for the order, so to speak, or it will exact a mental pledge, because its promise is not to be denied.

These rules are illustrated every day in many ways, for they apply equally to advertising in all media. Inevitably, taken together and carefully adhered to, they result in advertising that will command attention but never be offensive. It will be reasonable but never dull. It will be original but never self-conscious. It will be imaginative but never misleading. Because of these qualities it will make people act.

This is all I know about making advertising.

WILLIAM BERNBACH
Doyle Dane Bernbach

In **Madison Avenue, U.S.A.**, Martin Mayer said, "From Albert Lasker's day to the formation of Doyle Dane Berbach, no agency was willing to place memorability and originality over sales argument." William Bernbach stressed that the selling theme is important, but it is not enough. "You have to startle people into an immediate awareness of your advertising in such a way they will never forget it!"

. . . Everybody is doing research, everybody is coming up with the same answers, and all ads are looking alike.

Let me read you what I said on this subject about nine years ago at a 4A meeting: "Unless you were born into advertising with a lot of gold in your budget, you must be aware that not to be different is virtually suicidal. Why should anyone look at your ad? The reader doesn't buy his magazine or tune in his radio or TV to see and hear what you have to say. What brand of vanity or indifference leads us to believe that we can, so to speak, sit alongside world-shaking events and even be noticed? Our reader is confronted daily with history-making news. The papers are filled with sensationalism. The shocking news item is becoming a regular part of his news diet. With this deafening roar of frightening conflict beating about his ears, how do we expect him to hear our advertising story? How are we going to pierce this wall around him, this wall of violence? And if we pierce this wall, how are we going to get through that second wall, an almost impenetrable wall of competition crying its wares? Well, I suppose the constant shooting of coins against these walls will finally penetrate; but this is a long and costly way to attack.

"Now if you can't afford or are not willing to depend on the weight of a tremendous budget to crash through the walls of consumer resistance, then you must agree that the hackneyed, the passive, the trite doesn't stand a chance. Only a message with a tremendous vitality carried in a dramatic graphic treatment will ever reach your consumer. What's the use of saying all the right things in the world if nobody's going to read them? And believe me, nobody's going to read them if they are not done with freshness, originality and imagination." . . .

The most criminal waste of a company's money is that spent on advertising which the public is indifferent to, and that is going on all the time. You

Source: William Bernbach, "Some Things Can't Be Planned," a speech at the Western Regional Meeting of the American Association of Advertising Agencies, Pebble Beach, Calif., November 3, 1965.

can get the right theme. I can put down on a page a picture of a man crying, and it's just a picture of a man crying. Or I can put him down in such a way as to make you want to cry. The same research, virtually the same picture, but one will work and one won't work. The difference is artistry. The difference is the ability of a man to put it down in a way that will make you react in your gut. That's the difference.

LEO BURNETT
Leo Burnett Company

In 1961, Leo Burnett announced that his agency worked on the assumption that every product has "inherent drama." Once that drama has been found, it is one of the most interesting and believable of all advertising appeals. It is a natural "news" angle that people are interested in, and the prospective buyer receives at least an emotional reward for reading, listening to, or viewing the advertisement. "By inherent drama," said Burnett, "I mean putting a piece of red meat against a red background to express the virility of the meat."

I have always felt that perhaps the real key to this nebulous thing called "creativity" is the art of establishing new and meaningful relationships between previously unrelated things in a manner that is relevant, believable and in good taste, but which somehow presents the product in a fresh new light. . . .

One of the basic concepts in our shop is that there is what we call "inherent drama" in every product, and that our No. 1 job is to dig for it and capitalize on it rather than taking the easy way out and leaning on contrived devices and far-fetched associations. I don't think you have to be what they call "off-beat" to be interesting. A truly interesting ad or commercial is "off-beat" by its very rarity. . . .

Today we have both pictures and words at our command for the expression of this inherent drama, whether it is in a package of cigarettes or a high-priced automobile. The graphic arts have advanced so far, and with TV the predominantly visual medium that it is, I sometimes feel that good writing is rapidly becoming a lost art in advertising. . . .

As I have observed it, great advertising writing, either in print or TV, is always deceptively and disarmingly simple. It has the common touch without being or sounding patronizing. If you are writing about boloney, don't try to make it Cornish hen, because that is the worst kind of boloney there is. Just make it darned good boloney.

Source: Leo Burnett, "Keep Listening to that Wee Small Voice" [1961], in *Exploring Advertising*, eds. Otto Kleppner and Irving Settel (Englewood Cliffs, N.J.: Prentice-Hall, 1970), pp. 141–42, 144–45.

CAMPBELL-EWALD COMPANY

Several advertising agencies have built their creative philosophies around the advertiser's marketing objectives and advertising strategy. They contend that only after establishing this firm foundation can specific creative activities be initiated. Campbell-Ewald follows this approach, as stated in the agency's orientation presentation to creative trainees.

Do not start to make an advertisement until you understand the assignment.

Do not put pencil to paper until you understand the advertising problem.

Do your homework before you start to do any verbal or visual stunt-flying.

Study the marketing plan. Read the advertising objective. Steep yourself in the product or service proposition. Review the consumer research available to you. In short, decide what you want to say before you decide how to say it.

This may sound very basic. But it is all too easy to overlook the basics in a business that is both an art and a science. A copywriter or an art director can all too easily go ahead and make something that looks and sounds like an advertisement or a commercial—without knowing what is for sale and to whom. Studying before you start to make advertising need not stifle you. It will free you from making false starts. Doing your homework will only bring order to your originality, clarity to your cleverness, and credibility to your creative product.

ROSSER REEVES
Ted Bates & Company

One of the most enduring creative philosophies came from Rosser Reeves when he was chairman of Ted Bates & Company. In **Reality in Advertising,** Reeves presented the advertising world with a new concept called the ''Unique Selling Proposition''—or, as it is now widely known, the U.S.P.

What is a U.S.P.? Originated at Ted Bates & Company in the early 1940s, the theory of the U.S.P. enabled this agency to increase its billings from $4,000,000 to $150,000,000, without losing a client, while getting dramatic, and in some cases unprecedented, sales for its clients.

Today, U.S.P. is perhaps the most misused series of letters in advertising. It has been picked up by hundreds of agencies and has spread from country to country. It is now applied, loosely and without understanding, to slogans, slick phrases, strange pictures, mere headlines—in fact, to almost anything which some writers consider slightly different from what they find in competing advertisements. It is used with the casual looseness of Humpty Dumpty, in *Through the Looking-Glass,* when he said: ''When I use a word, it means just what I choose it to mean—neither more nor less.''

Actually, U.S.P. is a precise term, and it deserves a precise definition. So we will begin by saying that, like Gaul, it is divided into three parts:

1. Each advertisement must make a proposition to the consumer. Not just words, not just product puffery, not just show-window advertising. Each advertisement must say to each reader: ''Buy *this* product, and you will get *this specific benefit.''*

This admonition, of course, has been on page one of almost every advertising textbook for the past sixty years; but as you will see, it is becoming almost a lost art, and more honored in the breach than in the observance.

Source: Rosser Reeves, *Reality in Advertising* (New York: Ted Bates, 1960), pp. 45–46.

2. The proposition must be one that the competition either cannot, or does not, offer. It must be unique—either a uniqueness of the brand or a claim not otherwise made in that particular field of advertising.

One might assume that a unique proposition, in itself, would be a strong theoretical base for an advertisement. However, there are thousands of unique propositions that do not sell. Witness, a famous toothpaste once advertised: "IT COMES OUT LIKE A RIBBON AND LIES FLAT ON YOUR BRUSH." This was a proposition, and it was unique. However, it did not move the public, because it apparently was not of importance to them. So we come to the third part:

3. The proposition must be so strong that it can move the mass millions, i.e., pull over new customers to your product.

These three points are summed up in the phrase: "UNIQUE SELLING PROPOSITION."
This is a U.S.P.

DAVID OGILVY
Ogilvy & Mather

One of the most outspoken critics of advertising, David Ogilvy, attacked the assumption that every advertisement must do its own job of selling. He insisted that individual ads are contributions to a larger, long-term marketing program based on the product's "brand image." In his famous book on advertising, Ogilvy lists ten other "commandments" in which he emphasizes the importance of content over form, stresses the necessity of a good idea, and urges copywriters to "give the facts" but without either boring or merely entertaining the reader or viewer or listener: "The consumer isn't a moron; she is your wife."

Every advertisement should be thought of as a contribution to the complex symbol which is the *brand image*. If you take that long view, a great many day-to-day problems solve themselves.

How do you decide what kind of image to build? There is no short answer. Research cannot help you much here. You have actually got to use judgment. (I notice increasing reluctance on the part of marketing executives to use judgment; they are coming to rely too much on research, and they use it as a drunkard uses a lamppost, for support rather than for illumination.)

Most manufacturers are reluctant to accept any *limitation* on the image of their brand. They want it to be all things to all people. They want their brand to be a male brand *and* a female brand. An upper-crust brand *and* a plebeian brand. They generally end up with a brand which has no personality of any kind, a wishy-washy neuter. No capon ever rules the roost.

Ninety-five percent of all the campaigns now in circulation are being created without any reference to such long-term considerations. They are being created *ad hoc*. Hence the lack of any consistent image from one year to another.

What a miracle it is when a manufacturer manages to sustain a coherent style in his advertising over a period of years! Think of all the forces that work to change it. The advertising managers come and go. The copywriters come and go. Even the agencies come and go. . . .

The greater the similarity between brands, the less part reason plays in brand selection. There isn't any significant difference between the various

Source: David Ogilvy, *Confessions of an Advertising Man* [1963] (New York: Ballantine Books, 1971), pp. 87–90.

brands of whiskey, or cigarettes, or beer. They are all about the same. And so are the cake mixes and the detergents, and the margarines.

The manufacturer who dedicates his advertising to building the most sharply defined *personality* for his brand will get the largest share of the market at the highest profit. By the same token, the manufacturers who will find themselves up the creek are those shortsighted opportunists who siphon off their advertising funds for promotions. Year after year I find myself warning my clients about what will happen to their brands if they spend so much on promotions that there is no money left for advertising. . . .

A steady diet of price-off promotions lowers the esteem in which the consumer holds the product; can anything which is always sold at discount be desirable?

Plan your campaign for years ahead, on the assumption that your clients intend to stay in business forever. Build sharply defined personalities for their brands, and stick to those personalities, year after year. It is the total personality of a brand rather than any trivial product difference which decides its ultimate position in the market.

JACK TROUT
Ries Cappiello Cowell

In 1969, Jack Trout stated that the eras of the U.S.P. (Rosser Reeves) and the "image" concept (David Ogilvy) had passed. Each had been destroyed by the "me-tooism" of advertising agencies that followed Reeves in the 1950s and Ogilvy in the 1960s. In the 1970s, Trout said, advertisers would have to go further than they had before—namely, by engaging in "positioning."

Today's marketplace is no longer responsive to strategies that worked in the past. There are just too many products, too many companies and too much marketing "noise." We have become an overcommunicated society. . . .

Thousands of commercial messages compete daily for a share of the prospect's mind. And, make no mistake about it, the mind is the battleground.

To better understand what you are up against, consider the mind as a memory bank. Like a memory bank, the mind has a slot or "position" for each bit of information it has chosen to retain. In operation, the mind is a lot like a computer.

But there is one important difference. A computer has to accept what is put into it. The mind does not.

In fact, it's quite the opposite. The mind, as a defense against the volume of today's communications, screens and rejects much of the information offered it. In general, the mind accepts only new information which fits its previous pattern of slots or positions. It filters out everything else. And it doesn't make much difference how "creatively" the new information is presented. . . .

The computer "position" in the minds of most people is filled with the name of a company called "IBM." for a competitive computer manufacturer to obtain a favorable position in the prospect's mind, he must either dislodge IBM or somehow relate his company to IBM's position.

Yet, too many companies embark on marketing or communications

Source: Jack Trout, " 'Positioning' Is a Game People Play in Today's Me-Too Market Place," *Industrial Marketing,* June 1969, pp. 51–55.

programs as if the competitor's position did not exist. They advertise their product in a vacuum and are disappointed when their message fails to get through. . . .

Today, we are entering the positioning era. This will be an era that recognizes the importance of product features and the company image, but more than anything else stresses the need to create a "position" in the prospect's mind. . . .

If I've moved you to possibly consider your position, I'd like to offer you four simple rules for playing the game:

1. Find the people in your own organization and your agency who understand it. It's tough work and it's not played well by amateurs or non-believers. It is played well by people who have good marketing sense. It's also played well by people who have "vision." . . .
2. Be brutally frank about your product or company and its reputation. Try to eliminate all ego from the decision making. It clouds the issue. . . .
3. Change what you have to change. Take advantage of what you can take advantage of. Base these decisions on what's in the marketplace, not what's in the company. . . .
4. Establish your position and build a program around it that's big enough to get noticed.

THOMAS DILLON
Batten, Barton, Durstine & Osborn, Inc.

Batten, Barton, Durstine & Osborn (BBDO) started with the premise that there are two common sins in the execution of advertising: (1) creativity for the sake of technique and (2) no creativity at all. The first may get the message across, but probably not the right message and probably not aimed at the right consumers. The second may have a sound selling message, but it may bore you to death before you get it. On the basis of the BBDO premise, Thomas Dillon developed a creative philosophy designed to avoid these pitfalls.

Usually the intent of advertising persuasion is to influence a brand decision. . . . I believe that virtually every consumer sees and hears advertising in the full knowledge of that intent. How are brand decisions influenced by advertising? As I shall demonstrate, the purchase of any brand is usually stimulated by the consumer's desire to resolve a problem or complex of problems. . . .

The first step . . . of the creative process is to identify the prime prospect. Advertising is, after all, only a message, and a primary requirement in sending a message is identifying to whom it is to be sent. The prime prospect is defined as that group of individuals to whom the advertising should be directed. Usually they are high-frequency buyers who make the brand decision. . . .

The second step of the creative process is to determine what problems the prime prospect has in the category under consideration. . . .

The third basic step in the creative process is to examine the product or service in the light of what has been learned about the prime prospect and the problems involved in his decision process.

This usually requires the creative man having to personally involve

Source: Thomas Dillon, "The Creative Process," a speech given at the Federal Trade Commission's Hearings on Advertising, Washington, D.C., October 1971; reprinted as a pamphlet by BBDO.

himself with every detail of a manufactured product. . . . What he will try to do is visualize that product through the eyes of the prime prospect—not through the eyes of the technicians who make it. It is an important difference. . . . The assignment is to match up some set of the decision problems of the prime prospect with the characteristics of that product or service which will most likely lead to brand trial. . . .

At this point in our process, we will have developed what is called a copy concept. In simpler terms, this is a statement of what you hope the prime prospect will carry in her memory about your brand. It must be relevant to her decision. And yet it cannot be too complicated. The human mind is not designed to carry away a ream of engineering specifications that are irrelevant to the decision process. . . .

The next step is the execution of this copy strategy by executing, shall we suppose, a thirty-second TV commercial. In order to do this successfully, the commercial you prepare must accomplish the following: it must get the attention of the prime prospect; it must identify the domain of her decision; it must register the memory of your brand in this domain; it must register in her memory the content of the copy concept; and it must link the concept to the brand.

PART II
Copy

Chapter 1

Researching the Ad

Your assignment is to write an ad. Where do you begin? Most copywriters start with the verbal content of the ad, or the "copy"—that is, the headline, the subheadline, the body text, the signature, the caption, and the slogan. Few ads contain all these types of copy, but every ad contains at least one, and most ads use several.

Before you begin to write, however, you must do some preliminary work. Specifically, you must conduct research. You have to determine why you are writing, what you are writing about, and whom you are writing for.

Although there is no universally agreed upon method of answering these questions, there is some agreement on the importance of several stages or steps in the research process: (1) determine your prospects, (2) analyze your product, and (3) set your objectives.

Determine Your Prospects

Right from the start, it is imperative to know your audience. You need to find out who they are, what they want, and why they want it.

First, decide how you prefer to aim your message—with a shotgun at the mass market or with a rifle at a specific target market.

Consumers can be defined in terms of their relative actual or potential interest in the product or service you are offering. There are the hot prospects—those actively in the market for the kind of product your client is selling. There are the warm prospects—those who might be interested. Some of them won't know they're in the market until your ad catches their attention.

And that leaves the majority of consumers—those who are non-prospects. No matter how useful or inexpensive the product and no matter how effective or alluring the ad, these people are just not in the market for what you're selling. For example, you can't sell a maternity dress to a man or a retirement plan to a 70-year-old retiree.

Second, write a "consumer profile" for your product or service, describing your prospects as precisely as possible. Define them in terms of both demographics and psychographics.

Demographics

The quantifiable characteristics of any given human population are called "demographics." They include such factors as age, sex, income, education, occupation, and marital status. Demographics help the copywriter define the prospects as narrowly or as broadly as he or she chooses. Prospective consumers of the product might be all women, all persons over 50 years old, or all high school graduates.

More than likely, however, potential customers for a particular product will be more narrowly targeted: school-age girls from suburban middle-class families or under-30 married factory workers living in large cities and earning over $20,000 per year.

Psychographics

As incomes have grown and social mobility has increased, it has become more and more difficult to determine who will buy what strictly in terms of demographic factors. College teachers, professional musicians, and construction workers may have similar incomes, for example, but they also have different tastes and interests and, therefore, different buying habits.

The study of "psychographics" was developed to determine the more or less qualitative differences among people in the same demographic groups. This area of consumer research deals with such criteria as lifestyle, personal goals and values, and psychological traits. Markets defined psychographically might include bored housewives, sports-oriented businessmen, or teenagers who play computer games.

Analyze Your Product

Before you begin to write about your product or service, you should find out everything you can about it. Make up a "fact sheet" about the product, including its specifications (design, ingredients or materials, quality, workmanship, price), test results, sales records, and general information about the company that manufactured it.

Study and use the product yourself. Talk with salespeople, engineers, chemists, and dealers—anyone who might give you useful information. Go to the library and find out about the product category and about competitors' products. Read trade journals and books. Write to industry groups for research studies and reports. Determine the differences (both favorable and unfavorable) between your product and the products of your competitors. Investigate competitors' sales methods, advertising techniques, and marketing objectives.

In addition to this secondary research, conduct (or hire a firm to conduct) primary research, that is, direct investigations and analyses of consumers, including interviews and surveys. Usually, the purpose of such studies is to determine why consumers do or do not use your product. However, the subject of inquiry can be more specific. (For a sample fact sheet, see Exhibit 1-1.)

Set Your Objectives

Early in your preliminary thinking, you should decide what you want your ad to achieve or accomplish. If it is part of a larger advertising campaign or marketing plan, you must decide what role in this broader program the ad is to play.

EXHIBIT **1-1.**   Fact Sheet

foley's

ADVERTISING
FACT SHEET

DEPARTMENT NUMBER	DATE AD RUNS	LINES

ADV.#

ITEM _____ MODEL # _____

LIST FEATURES IN ORDER OF IMPORTANCE:

REG. PRICE (Temporary Reduction)	WAS (Permanent Reduction)	SALE PRICE

1.

2.

3.

SIZES: FABRIC CONTENT: COLORS:

LEAVE THIS SPACE FOR ADV. DEPT.

REASON FOR ADVERTISING MERCHANDISE:
☐ NEW LINE ☐ SEASON OPENING ☐ SALE ☐ SPECIAL PURCHASE ☐ CLEARANCE ☐ STAPLE STOCK

MERCHANDISE AVAILABLE:
☐ ALL 5 FOLEY'S ☐ DOWNTOWN ☐ SHARPSTOWN ☐ ALMEDA ☐ NORTHWEST ☐ PASADENA

CREDIT TERMS TO BE ADVERTISED:
☐ FEW PENNIES A DAY PLAN (IF SO, WHAT TERMS PER MONTH?) _____ ☐ FBA ☐ 30–DAY

ART INFORMATION:
☐ PICK UP ART FROM AD THAT RAN _____ ☐ TEAR SHEET ATTACHED ☐ GLOSSY ATTACHED

☐ MERCHANDISE WILL BE SENT TO ADVERTISING ☐ PHOTO ON FLOOR ☐ OTHER _____
LEAVE THIS SPACE FOR ADV. DEPT.

NOTE: MERCHANDISE TO BE ILLUSTRATED MUST BE IN ADV. DEPT. 2 WEEKS PRIOR TO THE WEEK AD RUNS:

VENDOR PAID? ☐ YES (PAID SLIP MUST BE ATTACHED) ☐ NO % _____ $ _____

WHAT REQUIREMENTS MUST BE MET TO AVOID A REVERSAL ☐ NAME IN HEADLINE ☐ NAME IN BODY COPY ☐ OTHER ____

WILL YOU ACCEPT PHONE AND MAIL ORDERS? ☐ YES ☐ NO   MAIL ORDER COUPON ☐ YES ☐ NO

QUANTITY ON HAND DATE AD RUNS _____ TOTAL RETAIL VALUE OF MERCHANDISE _____

DATE MERCHANDISE WILL BE IN STOCK _____ HAVE SIGNS BEEN ORDERED? ☐ YES ☐ NO

SUBMITTED BY: _____ DIV. MGR. APPROVAL _____
ADVERTISING DEPT.

The more specific you can be in stating your objectives, the easier it will be to write your ad. In fact, you shouldn't write a word of it until you have decided what you expect it to do.

Objectives can be broad or narrow. They can relate to either short- or long-range goals. They can concern products and services or ideas and images.

Retail Objectives

Objectives for retail advertisers tend to be oriented to immediate action. They should be more specific than objectives for national advertisers. Some common retail objectives are

- To draw traffic into the store
- To move out old merchandise in order to make room for new
- To create a store personality
- To identify the store with nationally advertised brands
- To bring in new customers
- To announce new lines or services

National Objectives

Advertising objectives for national advertisers usually are concerned with longer time periods as well as longer-lasting results. Some typical objectives for manufacturers include

- Introducing new products
- Supporting the sales force by obtaining inquiries
- Building the company image
- Announcing a product improvement
- Tying together a family of products
- Conveying the selling points and benefits of a product

ASSIGNMENT 1-1.   Don't Sell Me Things

People do not buy "things." They buy satisfactions of their wants and needs. For this reason, it is vital for the copywriter to look beyond the product itself to the motives of the people who buy it. The following passage illustrates the importance of analyzing consumer interests and attitudes, as well as product characteristics.

Don't sell me clothes. Sell me neat appearance. Style. Attractiveness.
Don't sell me shoes. Sell me foot comfort. The pleasures of walking on air.
Don't sell me furniture. Sell me an abode. Comfort, cleanliness, contentment.
Don't sell me books. Sell me pleasant hours. Profits of knowledge.
Don't sell me things. Please don't sell me things.

Complete each of the following sentences, indicating which needs and wants are associated with the products and services referred to.

1. Don't sell me tires. Sell me _____

2. Don't sell me life insurance. Sell me _____

3. Don't sell me a house. Sell me _____

4. Don't sell me dry cleaning. Sell me _____

5. Don't sell me a freezer. Sell me _____

6. Don't sell me bank services. Sell me _____

7. Don't sell me a deodorant. Sell me _____

8. Don't sell me a movie. Sell me _____

9. Don't sell me a pocket calculator. Sell me _____

10. Don't sell me a car. Sell me _____

Chapter 2

Preparing the Ad

After you have studied your product thoroughly, described your prospects precisely, and defined your objectives specifically, you still have to decide on the form and content of the ad. Again, although all copywriters develop their own way of proceeding at this point, several steps are indispensable: (1) write a copy platform, (2) develop a concept, and (3) choose an approach.

Write a Copy Platform

When you have gathered all the information available, work with it. Analyze it. Organize it. Pore over it again and again until you have gleaned from it every possible idea and combination of ideas you can find. As these ideas appear, rank them in order of importance. With this step, your creative thinking begins.

Now you are ready to develop a "copy platform," a written statement of objectives and summary of information for an ad or ad campaign. This planning statement is also called a copy plan, copy policy, or copy outline.

List your product's selling points (that is, product features such as raw materials, construction, colors, etc.) and its benefits (that is, user features that describe what the consumer gains from using the product—saves time, enhances beauty, is nutritious, etc.). Guidelines for preparing a copy platform are given in Exhibit 2-1.

Develop a Concept

Your copy platform gives you a summary of facts and a statement of goals, but it does not tell you which information to use and how to implement your objectives. For that purpose, you must develop a "concept"—that is, an idea or a thought that will help you in the selection and arrangement of ad materials.

The concept can be based on a particular service the product renders or on a particular need it satisfies. It can focus on physiological needs—for food, shelter, sex, or sleep—or on psychological needs—for security, status, or sex appeal. It can relate to the product's convenience, effectiveness, or quality. The concept can also be based on an association between the product and a desirable "state of being," such as love, success, freedom, or happiness.

The importance of a concept cannot be overstated. If your ad does not

EXHIBIT **2-1.** Copy Platform

Before you prepare any ad, you should work out a specific copy platform. While there is no standard copy platform format, the following list of questions should help you organize your information and your thoughts before you begin to write the ad.

1. Demographics: What specific groups and types of prospects are important?
2. What are the specific objectives—immediate and/or long run?
3. List all usable benefits, not just the ones to be used in the ad or current series of ads.
4. Positioning: Will the ad attempt to establish, maintain, or change current attitudes of prospects, or will it attempt to reinforce or change a product personality? In other words, how will this ad position the product in the mind of the consumer?
5. At what stage of its market history is this product now, and how does that affect the ad?
6. What will be the unique selling proposition—the keynote concept, the big idea?
7. What reinforcing benefits and proof will be presented?
8. What "nuts and bolts" (the necessary but promotional information) will be included?

derive from a unifying idea or an organizing thought, the most skillful writing in the world won't make it work. You may have to probe deeply before you come up with a usable concept. But find it you must. And after you find it, you must refine it. Simplify it. Strengthen it. You'll know when you've got it. And when you've got it, you're on your way!

Choose an Approach

After you have developed a concept, you must choose an appropriate approach for your ad. The choice depends partly on whether you want your ad to inform, persuade, or entertain—although it may perform more than one of these functions at the same time. Do you want to create interest? stimulate desire? establish conviction? induce action? Whatever the specific purpose of your ad—and in light of the concept you have developed—you have the following approaches to choose from.

Tone

The tone of an ad can be factual, emotional, or humorous. With a factual approach, you present the facts in a more or less straightforward manner. If your goal is to inform—especially about a reduced price, a free offer, a distinctive product feature, or an obvious consumer benefit—this may be the best way to create interest or induce action. The factual approach is also called "reason-why," "objective," "logical," or "descriptive."

The emotional approach appeals to the heart and the gut. It can involve the reader in the ad by dwelling on feelings—hopes, desires, and aspirations. If your purpose is to persuade, this method can be very effective. But it is also difficult to do well.

Humorous ads are, as the name suggests, intended to elicit anything from a smile to a guffaw. Like emotional appeals, ads using humor are not easy to write. And they should be used only if they are appropriate to the sales message and the product or service. Their primary goal is to create interest by entertaining.

Style

In terms of style—or *how* the ad is presented—there are several options: dramatization, demonstration, and presentation.

A dramatization or story is usually either emotional or humorous. It can stimulate desire or create interest by evoking a particular mood, such as nostalgia, togetherness, or escapism. A less atmospheric and more factual "slice-of-life" dramatization can establish conviction and induce action by both informing and entertaining. Also called "narrative."

A demonstration, usually factual in tone, shows how the product or service is used. It might consist of a description of the step-by-step operation of the product—say, an electric toothbrush or chainsaw, or a summary of the multiple uses of the product—say, a workbench or a set of kitchen utensils.

In a presentation, the features or benefits of the product are presented or described rather than dramatized or demonstrated. Almost always factual, presentations can also be humorous, particularly in the broadcast media, where some of the most popular presenters have been comedians and character actors.

Testimonials are presentations in which the presenter describes his or her firsthand experience with the product. The emphasis is usually on establishing conviction. This approach can be effective if the testimony is believable.

Other Options

Regardless of the style or tone of your ad, you might want to use a gimmick—that is, an unusual element or device. The copy might include a poem or a cliche. It might be handwritten, spelled out in toy blocks, or written in a foreign language. The usual purpose of such eye-catching techniques is to create interest, although the copy content—or illustration—might try to inform or persuade.

Usually copywriters decide on a format by selecting one style and one tone. However, in some cases, it is possible—and even desirable—to use more than one of either. The only guidelines are (1) use whichever approaches or formats seem useful and appropriate and (2) know which approaches you're using. That way, you can at least discover what works and what doesn't. And that discovery will help you choose more carefully next time around.

ASSIGNMENT **2-1.**   Choosing an Approach

Bring to class an example of each of the approaches to writing an ad discussed in this chapter: factual, emotional, humorous, dramatization, demonstration, and presentation. Include examples from both magazines and newspapers. Be prepared to defend the advertiser's reasons for the approach taken.

Chapter 3

Writing the Ad

At this point, you are ready to prepare a "creative strategy worksheet" (see Exhibit 3-1), which will allow you to bring together all your facts and ideas, including your thoughts on visualizing the ad (see Chapter 10). It will also help you plan a strategy for your product or service. It can be used as a guide for your creative thinking while you are finding solutions and as a rationale for your creative thinking after the solutions have been implemented.

Now—if you have done your homework—you are ready to begin writing. You have conducted your research, you have developed a strategy, and you have established a foundation on which to build your writing. Of course, it will be no easy task. The German philosopher Arthur Schopenhauer once said of creative writing: "There are three kinds of authors. First come those who write without thinking. Then come those who do their thinking as they are writing. Last of all come those who think before they write. They are rare." Be one of the rare ones. Decide first what you want to say. Then work on how you want to say it.

Write a Rough Draft

Begin writing your ad with the assumption that your first effort will be followed by several successive revisions. Consider it a rough draft that will only eventually be refined into finished and final copy.

A good starting point is to write a simple sentence that says what you want to say. Sometimes it is helpful to make the direct statement, "This advertisement is supposed to say ————." Then, you can begin to concentrate on how to say it forcefully, clearly, convincingly, and believably.

Although there are no hard and fast rules about what copy should include, there are some generally accepted guidelines. Regardless of your objectives, your concept, and your approach, you should (1) describe the product in terms of its benefits, (2) give complete, specific information, (3) use simple language, and (4) tell the reader to buy now.

Describe the Product's Benefits

A benefit is what the merchandise does for the user. "This jacket is made of windproof leather, snugly lined with lambswool." How many benefits are described in that sentence? The answer is—none. The sentence describes the product in terms of the product, not in terms of what it will do

EXHIBIT **3-1.** Creative Strategy Worksheet

Product (or Service): _____

Primary Selling Points: (Product Points: built-in characteristics of product itself, including any U.S.P.)

1. _____

2. _____

3. _____

Primary Benefits: (Prospect Points: what buyer gets from using the product or service)

1. _____

2. _____

3. _____

Consumer Profile of Target Prospect:

1. **Demographics:** (Age, sex, education, income, occupation)

_____

_____

2. **Psychographics:** (Lifestyle, attitude, personality traits)

_____

_____

Belief You Want This Ad To Establish:

_____

_____

Reasons Why Prospect Should Believe It:

1. _____

2. _____

3. _____

"Big Ideas" to Dramatize This Belief:

1. _____

2. _____

3. _____

Visualization of Big Idea:

1. Product alone: _____

2. Product in setting: _____

3. Product in use: _____

for the consumer. Windproof leather and lambswool lining are selling points, not benefits. Try this: "This jacket keeps you warm even in a gale at 20 below." There you have a benefit—that is, a description of what the product offers the prospective customer.

Give Complete Information

In writing retail ads, give enough information so the reader can pick up the phone and order the merchandise or drive to the store and buy it. Describe the product in detail, both to tell what it does and how it is different from competitors' products. "The chef's knife is 13½ inches long and has a 9-inch blade. It is used for heavy-duty cutting and slicing. It is especially good for carving meat."

Use Simple Language

Copy doesn't have to be fancy. In fact, it shouldn't be. Effective copy is completely lacking in self-consciousness and pretentiousness. It should avoid hackneyed adjectives and should make no exaggerated claims. You can be enthusiastic about your product, but you must not go overboard. To be convincing, you should write conversationally. That is, write the way you talk. In the hands of anyone but a skilled professional, this kind of writing can be flat and dull. But in the right hands, it can be both credible and comprehensible:

> Here's the story—round trip air fare from San Francisco to Freeport. Luxurious rooms at the King's Inn and Gold Club. Breakfasts and delicious dinners every day. Unlimited green fees at two golf courses and use of tennis courts. Tipping is included.

That's not fancy writing, but it is clear and convincing. That's because it is written in short, punchy phrases, using short, simple words.

Tell the Reader to Buy Now

Psychologists have discovered that, generally speaking, people like to be told what to do. Furthermore, they tend to do what they are told to do. So when you end an ad with a request for action, such as "Call now" or "Come in today," you're actually increasing the odds that people will respond to your offer. You're enhancing the ad's selling power.

Revise the Ad

Once you have composed a rough draft, you will have arrived at a beginning rather than an end. What you will possess is the raw material from which the final copy can be made. No professional writer is satisfied with his first, second, or even third draft. Usually it takes many more attempts to get it just right. So you must revise and revise. Then polish, polish, polish—right up to the deadline.

After the ad is written, look at it. Reread it carefully and critically. Make sure it achieves at least some of the following objectives:

Objectives	Means
A—command Attention	Headline, illustration, layout
I—sustain Interest	Subheadline, opening copy
D—create Desire	Copy
C—cause Conviction	Copy
A—instigate Action	Coupon, telephone number, address, action words

Your ad needn't do all these things at once, but, again, it should do some. And it should do the ones you want it to do. If it doesn't, revise it and rewrite it.

ASSIGNMENT 3-1.   Evaluating an Ad

Bring to class three newspaper ads and three magazine ads. Evaluate each in terms of the guidelines discussed in "Write a Rough Draft":

- Describe the products' benefits
- Give complete information
- Use simple language
- Tell the reader to buy now

Note: The ads you select should have at least 100 words of copy.

Chapter 4

The Headline

Many creative people in advertising believe that the most important element in an advertisement is the headline. Whether this can be proved or not is irrelevant. We know that many, if not most, readers do not read the body copy. If the reader doesn't read the body copy, he might, at least, remember something from a compelling and memorable headline. The headline must, therefore, communicate its message in lucid and comprehensible language. More specifically, its function may include the following:

- To stop the reader or, at least, attract his attention
- To stimulate interest in the proposition
- To lure readers into the body copy
- To select the prime prospects from the readers
- To summarize the selling message
- To identify the product or service
- To offer a benefit

Some copywriters create the headline before they write the body copy. Others do the headline after they've written the copy. It is suggested that the copywriter use the system he finds most productive.

There is no hard and fast rule about the length of headlines. They can range from one word, such as the notable headline for one of the earliest Volkswagen ads—"LEMON"—to David Ogilvy's famous 16-word headline for Rolls-Royce: "At Sixty Miles an Hour the Only Sound You Hear Is the Ticking of the Clock."

The Newspaper Advertising Bureau reminds us that writing an effective headline isn't easy and that sometimes copywriters in ad agencies may "write more than 100 headlines for a single ad." But since most advertising people don't have that much time to spare, here is a formula which may simplify the job.

A   for Attention
B   for Benefits
C   for Creativity

A for Attention

The readers whose attention you want are the ones in the market for the merchandise you have to sell. In the case of a single-item ad, this means that there are relatively few prospects who are in the market for your product.

Realistically, these are the only people you can sell anything to, and the objective is to get the attention of as many of them as possible. To do this, you can:

1. Call the prospect by name. If you're selling a golf and tennis tour, start your headline with "Golf and Tennis Buffs," or something similar. For a diet book, you might use just the word "Fat?" Headlines like these single out the prospect from the crowd and tell the prospect, "This is a message for you."

2. Talk the prospect's language. An ad headlined "Now . . . save on that new GE kitchen you've been saving for" talks the language of the woman who's been planning a new kitchen. And for the person who's just decided to get back into shape, the one word "Exercise!" is a great attention getter.

3. Use news in the headline. If something is new, say so. A headline like "New for men . . . the Arrow shirt that 'breathes' to keep you cool" is going to reach its target readers. So is "New in Smithville . . . the first great American small car."

4. Show the product in use. Always remember you've got an illustration working for you. If you show a man wearing a sports coat, you don't have to use the word "Men" in the headline to pick out your audience. Showing the product in use allows readers to picture themselves using it.

B for Benefits

Once you've gotten the attention of the right prospects, your headline should offer benefits. A benefit is what the product will do for the user. The headline, "New . . . the Arrow shirt that 'breathes' " is good as far as it goes. But it tells the reader only what the merchandise does. Much more effective would be this headline: "New . . . the Arrow shirt that 'breathes'—to keep you cool in 90 degree weather."

The fact that the shirt "breathes" is a selling point. The fact that it keeps you cool is a benefit. To figure out which benefits are most important to the prospect, the copywriter must look at the merchandise from the customer's point of view.

Here are a few effective headlines built around benefits:

For men's suits: "The single outfit from Palm Beach you wear five ways."

For a condominium: "Bayview Place townhomes have as much usable space as our big old house."

For a kitchen range: "This 30-inch gas range cleans itself continuously."

For a weight-loss center: "I lost it."

For office furniture: "Need office furniture fast? Is Thursday fast enough?"

For drapery: "Call shop-at-home now, and we'll bring our drapery and upholstery sale to you."

For kitchen redecorating: "A kitchen so beautiful your friends won't like it."

For a rug cleaner: "Steam clean method by Steven makes carpets and furniture look new."

C for Creativity

Creativity is the extra something that can turn a good headline into a great one. One of the most successful advertising campaigns of all time was headlined "Which Twin has the Toni?" In one year, it produced a 600 percent sales increase for Toni home permanents.

Why did this creative approach work so well for Toni? First, the ads used a large, dominant illustration aimed at getting the attention of the target audience: women interested in permanent waves. Second, the benefit—a permanent wave at home for a fraction of the cost at a beauty parlor—is presented intriguingly through the use of twins instead of two models who merely look somewhat alike. From that point on, the headline just about wrote itself.

Types of Headlines

Headlines, as we've seen, come in all shapes and sizes. There is no general agreement on how they should be classified. But most headlines fall into one of the following categories.

Presents news. Probably the most important and widely used type. People are interested in whatever is "new." Of course the product or its feature or benefit should be new. Words to use: "introducing," "now," "here," "at last," "finally," "today," "presenting," and "new."

Makes a claim. Requires a strong, emphatic statement that is, nevertheless, believable. Superlatives should be used sparingly and cautiously.

Offers advice. Uses the popular "how-to" approach. Also tells "why." Tends to set the advertiser up as an expert or authority.

Inspires curiosity. Reader is left wanting to know what's going on or how things will turn out. Often called "blind" or "gimmick." Conveys little or no product information.

Gives a command. Strong statement telling the reader to do something. Usually suggests action, a commonly desired result.

Offers a challenge. Urges the reader to do something. In strength of appeal, it is somewhere between advice (mild) and command (strong).

Identifies the product. Can be done by using a word, a phrase, a sentence, or a slogan. The word might be the name of the product or a reference to what it does or what need it satisfies. This kind of "label" is the weakest and least interesting of all the headline types, but it can be appropriate for well-known products.

When reputable research shows that many readers read the headline but not the body copy, it seems obvious that the headline should say something about the product or service. For that reason, it is astonishing how many headlines in newspaper and magazine ads fall into the "curiosity" or "blind" classification. And many of these are merely glib, whimsical, or clever.

The trouble is, they don't work. They are, in most cases, written by amateurs or novices who don't really understand what advertising is all about. Or they are the work of self-indulgent copywriters more interested in catering to their egos than to potential buyers.

Many young people are tempted to write the smart or tricky headline, in which nary a product benefit is mentioned—and nary a customer is collared.

The Slogan

Never underestimate the power of an effective, memorable slogan. For instance, if you mention the words "The Uncola," the first thing that comes to mind is 7UP. This simple two-word slogan has the power to relate an entire advertising campaign to the consumer.

A good slogan creates an image or a personality for a product or company and can be used repeatedly over a long period of time. Since the Seven-Up Company began using "The Uncola" slogan ten years ago, it has seen a jump in sales of over 100 percent.

"Prior to 1968, 7UP was thought of only as a specialty drink, mixer, or something to take for an upset stomach," says Keith Pickett, public relations spokesperson. Then came the great slogan campaigns—"The Uncola," "See the Light," and "Undo It." These variations of the same slogan created a new image in the mind of the American public. 7UP is no longer regarded as a bicarbonate, but as a soft drink in its own right.

Most businessmen, of course, are not trying to make their product a household word and aren't required to create a slogan as part of a multi-million-dollar campaign. Nonetheless, the objectives are the same as those of the corporate giant. In fact, the smaller the budget, the more a company needs the maximum possible impact for every dollar spent.

Unlike a print ad or broadcast commercial, a slogan can have tremendous staying power. It will be seen over and over again for as long as the advertiser uses it. Obviously, every advertiser has innumerable things he would like people to know about his product. But a good slogan is brief, concise, succinct. It says one thing. It makes one point. And it makes it well.

How do you create an effective slogan?

Personalize the message. To do this, an advertiser must clearly define his marketing objectives. Ideally, the product has been chosen to relate to a sales promotion and the copy line will relate to both the product and its promotional objective.

Be brief. It is better to say too little than too much. Try to avoid a cluttered look. To achieve impact and memorability, say it quickly and crisply.

Don't offend. Don't use words that automatically apply to only a portion of your market. Sexual innuendoes or slang words may offend part of your audience.

Stress consumer benefits. Self-serving puffery doesn't work. Instead, advertise a feature, service, or benefit.

When in doubt, sell. A really clever slogan might be talked about, but the best advertising copy doesn't call attention to itself; it calls attention to the product or the company.

Use the U.S.P. If you have a unique selling proposition, don't hide it. Use it. If the product has a truly unique, really different benefit or service, it can be a great advantage. Experiment with ways of saying it best, and if you come up with an effective combination of words, the result should be an appropriate and memorable slogan.

ASSIGNMENT **4-1.**   Making Headlines Fit

Journalists often are concerned with making headlines fit the space allotted from margin to margin. Headline writers, therefore, must develop broad vocabularies of multiple synonyms for common words.

For the common words below, list synonyms with the number of letters specified. (Note: words are used as verbs.)

1. Announce   (6) _____   (5) _____   (4) _____

2. Approve   (7) _____   (6) _____   (4) _____

3. Ask   (7) _____   (5) _____   (4) _____

4. Delay   (8) _____   (6) _____   (5) _____

5. End   (8) _____   (6) _____   (4) _____

6. Give   (7) _____   (6) _____   (5) _____

7. Honor   (7) _____   (6) _____   (4) _____

8. Name   (7) _____   (6) _____   (4) _____

9. Need   (7) _____   (6) _____   (4) _____

10. Plan   (6) _____   (5) _____   (4) _____

11. Reject   (7) _____   (6) _____   (4) _____

12. Report   (7) _____   (6) _____   (5) _____

13. Say   (6) _____   (5) _____   (4) _____

14. See   (6) _____   (5) _____   (4) _____

15. Seek   (6) _____   (5) _____   (4) _____

16. Study   (8) _____   (7) _____   (5) _____

17. Support   (6) _____   (5) _____   (4) _____

18. Take   (6) _____   (5) _____   (3) _____

19. Want   (7) _____   (6) _____   (4) _____

20. Win   (7) _____   (5) _____   (4) _____

ASSIGNMENT **4-2.** Writing Headlines for Ad Copy

There is no specified time that headlines have to be written. Sometimes they are written before the copy and sometimes after. Often, when the body copy already has been written, the headline is there for the finding. Sometimes a thought is paraphrased for the headline. Always study your copy for headline ideas.

Read the following passages, then write three (3) headlines for each. Circle the number of the one you think is best for each passage.

A. Capital National Bank

For a safe investment plus a high rate of interest, look into certificates of deposit. At Capital National Bank. Unlike other rates, rates on certificates of deposit under $100,000 are not affected by today's fluctuating economic conditions. So you can deposit a minimum of $1,000, then just sit back and earn a guaranteed interest rate of 7¼% for 4 years. Or 7½% for 6 years. Capital will pay you the interest quarterly, with your choice of payment plans. These include compounding the interest on your certificate, crediting your Capital savings or checking account with the interest earned, or, if you prefer, a cashier's check. In addition, all deposits are insured up to $100,000 by the FDIC. Remember, when it comes to good investments, all you need is Capital. And we've got the certificates to prove it.

1. _____

2. _____

3. _____

B. Leon's Shoes

Give us 60 seconds alone with your feet! Try on a pair. Walk around. Not just on carpet—walk around on a hard surface. Feel how light, how flexible they are. You'll discover a new experience in comfort. It's all in the sole, made of "molecules of air." And that's what you walk on. Once you try them you'll understand. From $45 in multiple colors. Use your charge cards.

1. _____

2. _____

3. _____

C. Joske's

Roxanne brings you exciting new swimsuits so supple and lightweight they feel like a "second skin"! Bra-sized to make the most of your figure in a body-hugging blend of Antron nylon and Lycra spandex. From $26 to $32 in several styles and colors. See them all in Swimwear. Highland Mall. And charge it.

1. _____

2. _____

3. _____

D. Ken-L Ration's Cheese-Flavored Burger

Does your dog like the flavor of cheese? Just get some cheese out of the refrigerator and give your dog a taste. If he's like other dogs he'll love cheese. That's why we made new Ken-L Ration Cheese-Flavored Burger. It has real cheese right in it. And it's completely nourishing . . . with all the protein, all the minerals, all the vital nutrients your dog needs. Ken-L Ration Cheese-Flavored Burger has cheese. And dogs love cheese.

1. _____

2. _____

3. _____

Chapter 5

Copyediting

After you have rewritten your ad, checked it against your objectives, and verified its contents, you must make sure it is correct in terms of grammar, capitalization, punctuation, spelling, and so on. Also, you might want to make some last-minute changes in word choice or add or delete material. This task is called "copyediting." It can be performed on your own ads or, if you are a copyeditor, on the ads submitted to you by copywriters.

Ordinarily, you should follow the rules set forth in the editorial style sheet of your newspaper or magazine. Of course, advertising style is not strictly bound by editorial guidelines written for news reporters and features writers. However, you should be familiar with the rules and depart from them only for good reasons. If your writing style is ungrammatical or otherwise faulty, don't use "creativity" as an excuse. Learn the rules, follow them, and forget them only when you know why you are doing so.

Memorize the list of copyediting symbols in Exhibit 5-1. Then use them in the copyediting exercises that follow. Their purpose is to allow copyeditors—or copywriters editing their own writing—to revise without retyping and to communicate changes to the typesetter or compositor in a universally understood editorial shorthand.

EXHIBIT **5.1** Copyediting and Proofreading Symbols

Paragraphing

Begin paragraph	¶ or ⌐ Once upon a time
Don't paragraph	No¶ Once upon a time
Run together	were married. ⌐ Later they were

Typography

Set in Roman	Rom
Set in italic	Then look first
Set in caps	White, green, blue
Set lower case	Spring
Set boldface	Ultra-modern

Punctuation

Insert period	etc⤬ or etc⊙
Insert comma	red, white, blue
Insert semicolon	and fun, then the
Insert colon	following, Jim, Jack
Insert apostrophe	You don't say
Insert quotes	said, "Go away!"
Insert leaders	very happy ⤬⤬⤬⤬
Insert dash	tiered⊦two on top
Insert hyphen	likewise (or =)
Insert question mark	Why not?

Spacing

Put in space	percent
Close up	Best Bilt
Delete & close up	has been fair

Insertion and Deletion

Insert word	discover ∧ now what this (right)
Delete & close	This small book
Delete & close	colours
Leave as was	This small book stet

Position

Transpose order	to swiftly go
Transpose order	freindly
Move to left	Beginning
Move to right	ending.
Center	Here it is
Move up	
Move down	

Abbreviation

Abbreviate word	horsepower
Spell out word	h.p.
Put in figures	fifty-six
Spell out	3

Instructions

More copy, another page	more
Second page of copy	Add 1
Third page of copy	Add 2
End of copy, no more	# # # # or -30-

	Name
	Lab
ASSIGNMENT **5-1.** A Copyediting Exercise	Date

Read the following paragraphs carefully. Indicate errors (if any), using the symbols in Exhibit 5-1.

It takes a lot of courage to take this course. It's companant parts are varied and complex and its going to be inordinately difficult unless I listen attentively and absorb. In so far as my writing is concerned, I may think I'm proficient and that its alright, but it probably still requires a lot of attention. In as much as I'm open minded, I'll take what comes, subdue my ego and hope for the best. Its a real challenge.

I know that I have an ocassional tendancy to mispell words but any body can do that. It is, I think a minor transgression and not too hienous an offence.

There are other egregious offences I will strive to avoid, knowing that I will go farther in this course if I adhere to a few basic rules. I will attempt to be clear, concise and succinct. I will avoid exclamation points for they are jejune, and the mark of a lazy and incompetent writer. I will avoid the use of words ending with ''ize'' (such as ''finalize). Why? Because they are fuzzy, silly and puerile. I will try to remember that there is something called a ''paragraph''.

But irregardless of what ensues, like too much home assignments I trust the Prof realizes that none of us are perfect.

ASSIGNMENT **5-2.**   Editing National Copy

Copyedit the following national ad, using the copyediting symbols in Exhibit 5-1.

Headline: How Admiral Byrd and the South Pole Helped Make Longines the World's Most Honored Watch

"After the remarkable results ob tained by longines timing equipment I can only choose Longines for exact the timing of my second antartic expedition. For many years my Longines Chronograph watch has never left my armm and has been my faith ful companion. I always rely on Longine's accuracy". He carried fifty :pngenes timing instruments on Expedition II. Even his dog sleds were equiped with Longines chronometers as a safty measure? All the original aerial maps of this unchartered continent, were made with the help of Longines navigation equipment. Byrd, himself, lived totally alone for 5 months, depending entirly upon the reliabiliyt of his equipment. Longines ewatches are built to last; so Longines uses onyl the finest jewels and metals. Cuts them with amazing precision and puts them together with diligent care. All parts are scrupulusly tested before assembely. Theh retested. And again? Inspection after inspection insures a beautifuly working watch. And pretects against the micro scopic imprefections and burrs who cause friction, the thief of accuracy. Longines has honered been with 1st prises for accuracy the world over. Longines.

ASSIGNMENT **5-3.** Editing Local Copy

Copyedit the following retail ad, using the copyediting symbols in Exhibit 5-1.

Headline: Bill Brewer Has Marketing Plans for Citizens

Bills the new Vice President for Marketing at citizens National Bank. Hes a new man? In a new position. And he's got a lot of dynamic new ideas. "forming the position of Vice president for marketing represents a concept new for Citizen's," Bill explains, "a more flexible aggressive approach to business developemnt. It goes beyondd advertising and public relations to major credit cards, person to person business development, even the busi ness Citizens' does with other banks". Thats alot to handle. And Bill Brewer has the ability and back ground to do it." Bill's lived in Austin all his life. So he heally knows the community. He graduated from the University of Texas with a BBA in finance and then served as cash control cfficer in the army finance corps. After service the, he spent ten years with 1 of Austins' largest downtown banks in commercial loans and busyness developement and public relations. So bill knows the bank ing business two. "A bank is here to help people", Bill says. "At least Citizens is. And the secret to marketing our services is to find out how we can help". Bill also feels responsable for informing the community of Citizen's specific services. He remarks, "One of my major goals is to use our advantages to help the Austin business community." And Bill brewer will do it. Hes a good example of how our people at Citizens National are willing to help.

ASSIGNMENT **5-4.**   Brevity in a National Ad

Long copy is quite appropriate and effective in many ads, as is shown by the example below. But situations might arise that require the copy to be cut in length, such as to fit into a smaller space.

In the copy below, reduce the number of words by about half. You still must retain the original message and flavor. Cut out words directly on the copy below. Then rewrite the copy with your suggestions, adding words necessary for smoothness. Finally, retype it and submit it to your instructor.

Incidentally, the headline for the ad is:

"I burned my business to the ground.
Thanks, America, for helping pay for it."
—Anon.

Arson fires cost over $1 billion last year. Who pays for this billion dollar bonfire? We *all* do.

When somebody decides to put a match to his business it is tough to prove. When arson for profit can't be proven, the insurance company has no choice but to pay. All of us contribute to these soaring damage claims by paying more for our own property insurance. Because insurance is merely sharing a risk among many.

What can you do about it?

Help to have arson classified as a major crime. One with the same high priority for prosecution as robbery.

Push for uniform state laws on reporting, detection and investigation. Laws that would make arson harder to get away with. (Over 20% of all fires are thought to be arson, yet only 1%-3% of confirmed arson cases result in conviction.)

Work for programs to improve investigation techniques and cooperation among fire fighters, police officers and insurance investigators.

Write to state officials.

Tell insurance commissioners, police and fire department officials that you would like to see some changes made.

Put pressure on local prosecutors and encourage them to get involved.

Let people know you've had enough.

Send for our "Enough is Enough" consumer booklet. It's full of information on the causes and the pro's and con's of some possible cures for high insurance rates. You'll find out how to register your views where they count. And how you can help hold down your own insurance costs.

Or you can just do nothing and figure the problem will go away. Of course if it doesn't, better keep you checkbook handy.

Enough is Enough

Write The St. Paul for your "Enough is Enough" booklet. Or contact an Indpendent Agent or broker represening The St. Paul. He's in this with you and wants to help. You'll find him in the Yellow pages.

St. Paul Fire and Marine Insurance Company, 385 Washington St., Saint Paul, MN 55102

The St. Paul Property & Liability Insurance.

ASSIGNMENT **5-5.**   Brevity in a National Ad

In the copy below, reduce the number of words by about half, but retain the original message and flavor. Cut out words directly on the copy below. Then rewrite it with your suggestions, adding words necessary for smoothness, and retype it to be turned in, if instructed to do so.

Executive Timber by Hallmark

Executive Timber is wood, carefully and expertly crafted into superb writing instruments.

Take the pen in your hands. Feel the heft of it. The warmth of it. Roll the barrel between your fingers. Note the subtle texture of the grain, enriched by fine Swedish oils.

Because no two grain patterns are precisely alike, every pen and pencil in the Executive Timber line is unique. You will own an original. One of a kind.

Executive Timber. A distinguished gift. An intensely personal possession. So carefully created Hallmark gives you a lifetime guarantee against even the slightest mechanical defect.

Executive Timber is for the person who likes the feel of wood—the warmth of wood—and the naturalness of wood.

There's walnut, richly grained and deep in color, from the timberlands of North America.

There's teakwood, as robustly colorful as the teakwood that graced the majestic sailing ships of the 1800's.

There's wenge from the African Congo—perhaps the most distinctively grained wood in the world.

There's cordia, hard and finely-textured, from the East Indies.

And rosewood. And tulipwood. Both imported from the rain forests of South America.

Each of these woods has its own personality. Its own grain pattern. Its own color. Its own texture. And for the discerning craftsman, each of these exotic woods has its own distinctive musk.

The pen writes as comfortably as it feels. Glide it over a sheet of fine paper and notice how the tungsten carbide point leaves a smooth, single-width marking.

A sealed cartridge resists the possibility of leakage—even if you are 3000 feet up and traveling at 650 miles an hour.

For those reasons and more, every Hallmark Executive Timber product carries a lifetime guarantee against even the slightest mechanical defect. This guarantee is backed by every store that sells Executive Timber. The promise is simple and clear: any mechanical defect will be promptly corrected at no cost to you.

Executive Timber. A distinguished gift. A prized possession. Perhaps the most prudent purchase you will make this year.

Pen and pencil set $30. Pen $15. Pencil $15. At fine stores where quality writing instruments are sold. Hallmark Cards, Inc., Kansas City, Mo.

ASSIGNMENT **5-6.**   Brevity in a Local Ad

The following ad uses long copy. Cut the copy in half, but retain the primary message. Funds have been reduced, and the ad must run shorter. Use this sheet as a worksheet. Recopy the finished ad on a separate sheet.

Headline: There's a Bonus in the Attic. And in the Price.

Remember the attic? It's usually right over the garage, accessible through a tiny hole and pull-down ladder (if you're lucky). Packed with empty boxes, last year's Christmas decorations, cobwebs. And a lot of wasted space.

Bring on the Bonus Room. Now instead of the dark, spooky attic, there's a big 20-foot by 14-foot windowed room, blanketed in toe-deep shag, brightened by soaring vaulted ceilings, and just a hop, skip and a turn up the staircase. It's a perfect playroom for the kids, a pool room for Dad, or a nice, quiet hobby center for Mom.

1,452 sq. ft. for $95,500. And the Bonus Room's not all you get. Take a look at the floorplan. Party-sized living room with fireplace, windowed dining room, three healthy bedrooms, two full baths, enclosed garage, and plenty of giant walk-in closets. Plus the old-fashioned Milburn quality. Hand-finished woodwork, marble vanities, hand-laid tile baths, plush carpeting, and money-saving Natural Energy appliances and central heating and cooling. (And you still get an attic. Only this one has a door opening to it off the Bonus Room. Easy to get to. And just the right size.)

See today in two great locations. Beacon Ridge: a quiet, secluded community of homes near schools and shopping. Furnished models open daily till dark. And Meadow Creek: an exclusive recreational community with its own swimming pool, hike and bike trails, and wooded greenbelts. Homeowner fee of only $10 a month gives you and your guests unlimited use.

The Bill Milburn Company. Building new homes the old way.

Chapter 6

Copyfitting

Copyfitting is the matching of copy and space. Usually, it refers to determining how much space will be needed to accommodate a given piece of copy. But it also can refer to determining how much copy will be needed to fill a given space. Both situations are common in advertising.

There are three basic approaches to copyfitting. The *square-inch* method is the simplest, but the least accurate. It is used mainly to approximate. The *word-count* method is more accurate, but takes more time and still results only in an approximation. The most accurate method of copyfitting is the *character-count* approach. It requires use of a special table that gives characters-per-pica (CPP) counts for various typefaces.

Before each of the three copyfitting methods can be explained, several key units of measurement must be defined. Used in typography and printing, they should be committed to memory by advertising people intending to work in and around advertising graphics and production, including copy and layout.

$$1 \text{ inch } = 72 \text{ points}$$
$$1 \text{ pica } = 12 \text{ points}$$
$$6 \text{ picas } = 1 \text{ inch}$$

Since most typewriters are designed to produce six single-spaced lines per inch, each line must measure approximately one pica.

Square-Inch Method

The square-inch method of copyfitting is based on the average number of words per square inch in a known type size already set. The procedure is rather simple:

1. Find a piece of copy already set in the face, style, and size desired.
2. Measure a minimum 10 individual one-inch squares with a ruler.
3. Count the words in each square, then average the 10 squares, giving the average number of words in a square inch.
4. From this, you can determine approximately how many words will fill a given space on a layout, or how much space will be taken by given typewritten copy. Simply count the words and measure the space.

Word-Count Method

The word-count method is based on the fact that in standard typefaces the average word occupies three ems of any given type size, in 10-point type or smaller. (An em is the square of the type size.) Eleven-point type or larger takes up slightly less space (2½ ems). To determine the space needed for 3 ems of a given typeface, multiply the type size by 3. For example, the 8-point em is 8 points on each side. So, for this type size, the "average word conversion" would be 8 × 3, or 24 points. This method of calculation does not work for condensed or expanded type. To figure out how many words will fit a given space,

1. Multiply the type size by 3 (if 10-point or under).
2. Determine the length of line desired, in inches.
3. Convert it to points by multiplying by 72 (72 points per inch).
4. Divide line length by average word length to get *average words per line*.

From typewritten copy to space it will fill

5. Divide words per line into total words to get total number of lines.
6. Figure depth of space by multiplying lines times point size plus any leading between each line.

From given space to number of words needed

5. Figure depth in points (inches times 72 points per inch).
6. Divide depth in points by type size plus leading between lines to get number of lines.
7. Multiply number of lines times number of words per line to get total number of words needed to fill the given space.

Character-Count Method

The most accurate copyfitting method involves knowing the total number of characters in the copy, either already written or to be written. It also requires a characters-per-pica chart, which is available from most typographers and printers.

Finding Space to Fit Given Copy

You must decide on one of the two dimensions, width or depth. Both cannot be left unknown. For example, if the width is decided upon, and the problem is to determine the depth,

1. Determine total number of characters in manuscript. (The simplest method is to count characters in the shortest line and multiply by the number of lines. Then count and add all the characters to the right of that point. Include spaces in the count.)
2. Determine the CPP figure for your typeface and size. (Refer to the characters-per-pica chart.)
3. Determine the number of characters per line. (Multiply CPP times the width you decide on, in picas.)

4. Determine the number of lines. (Total characters divided by characters per line.)
5. Determine total points deep. (Number of lines times type point size, with leading desired between lines added.)
6. Convert points deep to picas (divide by 12) or inches (divide by 72).

Finding Number of Typewritten Lines to Fill Given Space

In this situation, you have a given space and want to know how much copy you need to fill it. This problem requires that you know how many lines of typewriting will be needed.

1. Determine depth of given space in points. (If in inches, multiply by 6 picas; then by 12 points. If in picas, multiply by 12.)
2. Determine number of lines of printed type. (Divide points deep by type point size, including leading.)
3. Determine number of characters per line. (Multiply characters per pica by given width of space.)
4. Determine total number of characters in space. (Multiply characters per line by number of lines.)
5. Convert total characters to number of typewritten lines needed. (Divide total number of characters by an average line length to set on your typewriter, which you decide on.)

ASSIGNMENT 6-1.   Copyfitting

Using the character-count method, figure the depth of the copy below if typeset 10/12 Helvetica, 18 picas wide. (Use CPP count 2.6.)

If you love really fine furniture and up-to-the-minute decorating and won't accept anything less for your home, you'll love Caiati, America's largest showcase center for famous Drexel Heritage furniture.

Whatever the decor, at Caiti you'll find the perfect piece or grouping to give any room the rich, distinctive look that turns ordinary into extraordinary. From bedrooms to bookcases. Divans to dining rooms. A world of accessories. Plus, famous Karistan carpet, and beautifully coordinated custom draperies . . . those often over-looked finishing touches you need to create true harmony in a home.

And, Caiti offers some very important "extras" you're not likely to find elsewhere. Like prompt personal attention by our staff of professional decorator/designers (it's complimentary of course). Fast, on-time delivery on hundreds of items from our huge inventory. A pleasant, relaxed atmosphere without pushing crowds or pushy salesmen. All part of Caiti's unmatched service . . . a tradition for more than 64 years.

But why not see for yourself? If you're shopping for the finest in furniture, come to Caiti, you owe yourself a visit.

Depth _____

ASSIGNMENT **6-2.**   Copyfitting

Select a typeface and size for the following copy so that it will fit in a space 12 picas wide by 28 picas deep.

From early attic to Texas funky, the decor at The Old Spaghetti Warehouse is anything but coordinated chic. It's uncommonly fun!

Where else could you have dinner in an honest-to-goodness trolley car. Or an old-timey brass bed?

But the decor is only one reason families keep coming back time after time to The Old Spaghetti Warehouse.

Our menu and prices have a lot to do with our popularity.

From spicy chili to meatballs in tomato sauce. From tender clam to tangy cheese sauce, our spaghetti dinners with ten different sauces are a taste sensation. And all for under $3.

Our baked lasagne, chicken Pettazini, and breaded veal Parmigiana are under $4. And all entrées at The Old Spaghetti Warehouse are served with a fresh Italian salad and all the hot San Francisco sourdough bread you can eat!

We can't think of a single place you get more for your money. So bring the whole family! But don't expect the chairs to match.

Typeface _____   Size _____

PART III
Layout

Chapter 7

Elements

The layout is the blueprint or plan of an advertisement. It shows which elements the ad will include, how they will be arranged, and—roughly—what the finished ad will actually look like.

Generally, designing an effective layout should follow the guidelines for writing effective copy. It must attract and hold the attention of the reader or viewer, help him or her go through the ad, and communicate everything it is supposed to communicate.

Specifically, the layout (1) shows the size and shape of the ad as it will finally appear, (2) indicates the spatial relationships among the elements in the ad, and (3) gives everyone involved a chance to edit, review, and criticize it. The layout also helps the layout artist organize his or her thinking.

The designer of an ad must decide which elements to use before he decides how they will appear on the page. The main elements are illustration, typeface, white space, and color, as well as body copy, headline, slogan, logo, and price.

Illustration

Merchandise ads without illustrations are usually less noted and read than those with illustrations. For people who are shopping the ads, the picture can be as important as the words. In fact, ads with illustrations covering 50 percent or more of the ad space usually get better readership than those with smaller illustrations.

Be sure to choose an illustration style that is within the advertiser's means. And make sure that it will reproduce well in your newspaper or magazine. But avoid shifting from one style to another. A consistent style is one of the most important aspects of effective illustration.

Typography

The typeface or faces you select should be appropriate for the product or store, especially the display faces, and should be as distinctive as possible. However, blending several typefaces for a harmonious effect is a job for an artist or a type expert. If neither is available, limit yourself to one typeface for headlines, subheads, and prices and another typeface for body copy. For extra emphasis and variety, you can use different sizes, boldface, and italics within your two basic faces.

Body copy should be set in a clear, easy-to-read typeface, in a size at least as large as the type in your news columns—and preferably larger. Body copy should rarely, if ever, be set in reverse or surprinted over a picture or screen. Surprinting and reverse aren't particularly effective for headlines and display type either.

White Space and Color

The portion of the ad not occupied by either illustration or copy is called "white space." Properly used, white space can give an ad an image of elegance and the product it displays an image of quality. It also helps the ad stand out on the page, which is usually crowded with type. Of course, how much white space you use will depend partly on how much information you have to convey. If the illustration is fairly detailed and/or the copy contains much indispensable data, white space will have to be minimized.

A little color can make an ad stand out on a page in an impressive and eye-catching manner. In fact, adding one color to a black-and-white ad can greatly increase readership. Color also adds excitement—and recognition—to a store's ads. However, you have to weigh the advantages of using color against the extra cost.

Price

In national advertising, most ads do not include the price. The reason is obvious; the manufacturer does not dictate to the retailer what he may or may not charge. In local advertising, however, people expect and want to see the price. Almost all stores, whether huge supermarkets, swanky department stores, or small neighborhood shops, feature price. In these cases, price is an important (and often a dominant) element in the layout of retail ads. In fact, many local advertisers build their ads around price.

Slogans

A slogan can be an integral component of an advertising campaign. If it identifies the advertiser and is memorable, a slogan can act as a continuing link in a campaign. It acts as a constant reminder, provides recognition, and gives continuity. Advertisers are reluctant to change an effective slogan and may use the same one for many years or even decades. Some products (cigarettes, perfumes, etc.) use the slogan as a headline to the exclusion of all other copy.

Logotypes

The logotype, usually referred to as the "logo," is the name of the advertiser in a particular type or art form that remains constant from one ad to the next. A closely related term—"signature," or "sig"—is often used synonymously with logo, although it actually means the name of the advertiser in any form. Unlike the logo, it may change form from one ad to another.

Chapter 8

Materials

Because doing layouts requires drawing, cutting, and pasting, you will need special materials for performing these tasks. The primary layout materials are:

- Tracing pad (14" × 17")—Strathmore, Graphics, Ad Art
- Felt-tip marker (narrow)—black
- Felt-tip marker (wide)—black, red, blue, yellow, green, gray
- Typing paper (8½" × 11")—white
- X-acto knife
- Rubber cement (4 oz. bottle)
- Graphic arts ruler
- Eraser—kneaded
- Pencils—No. 2
- Liquid paper
- Roll masking tape
- Scissors

To accomplish neat and accurate layouts, it is also necessary to have a drawing table, a T-square, and a triangle (see Exhibit 8-1). Even if they are available in the lab, you may want to purchase an inexpensive drawing board and T-square for use at home. Practice with them until you are good and fast.

Drawing board or table. Preferably, your drawing surface should be smooth and adjustable both in height and angle. It should have at least one perfectly straight edge, usually the left edge for right-handed persons and the right edge for left-handed persons. If the board has a metal edge, it will be more accurate and will allow the T-square to slide more easily.

T-square. 24-inch. Preferably metal. Other materials (particularly plastic) do not hold their squareness as well, and you cannot cut along them with a knife without damaging the edge. Never use a knife on a plastic T-square.

Triangle A 10-inch, 30/60-degree, or a 6-inch, 45-degree triangle is used in combination with a T-square to draw vertical lines.

Tracing paper allows you to trace without a backup light. But you may not have any, or you may want to see more detail than such paper reveals. In such cases, you will need a light table—a piece of glass, large enough and thick enough for you to write on, with a light behind it. If you don't have a light table, use your imagination. You probably have makeshift light tables all over your house or apartment. Of course, you could buy a piece of heavy glass, tape the edges, and have your own portable light table.

Exhibit **8-1.**   Using a Drawing Board

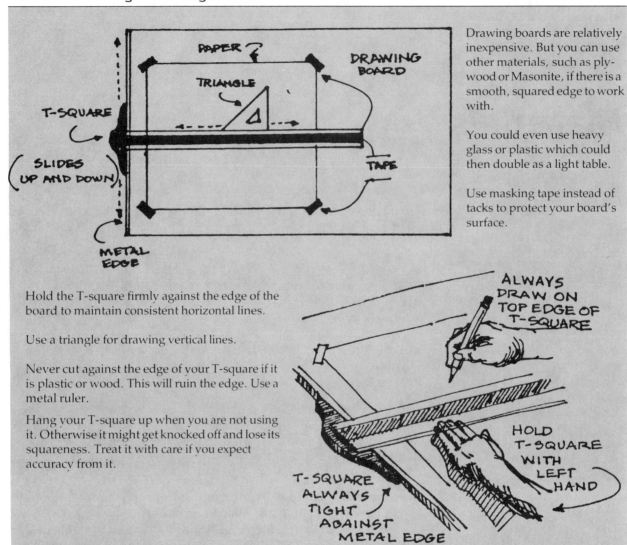

Drawing boards are relatively inexpensive. But you can use other materials, such as plywood or Masonite, if there is a smooth, squared edge to work with.

You could even use heavy glass or plastic which could then double as a light table.

Use masking tape instead of tacks to protect your board's surface.

Hold the T-square firmly against the edge of the board to maintain consistent horizontal lines.

Use a triangle for drawing vertical lines.

Never cut against the edge of your T-square if it is plastic or wood. This will ruin the edge. Use a metal ruler.

Hang your T-square up when you are not using it. Otherwise it might get knocked off and lose its squareness. Treat it with care if you expect accuracy from it.

Chapter 9

Illustration

The advertising illustration, either a photograph or a drawing, is designed to attract the reader's attention. Combined with other elements, it can create a strong visual impact—much stronger than the impact of any of the elements used alone.

Guidelines

To achieve this objective, however, the illustration must be thematically related, properly composed, and effectively positioned.

The illustration should tie in with the copy—especially the headline. The people in it should be those who—by sex or age or appearance—would be likely to use the product. They should be dressed appropriately for what they are doing. The background should complement and support rather than overwhelm or detract from the foreground figures: the product itself or the people using the product.

When chosen carefully and handled properly, an illustration can call attention to the ad by making it visually appealing: attractive, entertaining, or interesting.

Photographs or Drawings?

The decision to use either a photograph or a drawing depends on several considerations. Art work can be made to create the exact mood desired for the advertisement. Various aspects of the illustration can be more easily controlled and manipulated. Also, art work seems to be more effective when the ad deals with abstractions, such as political ideas, space exploration, and energy conservation, or with services rather than products.

On the other hand, most readers find it easier to identify with actual objects than with drawn figures. In fact, this is why photographs of people and products are used in so many ads. A good photograph can convey believability and credibility. Furthermore, a photograph can illustrate a demonstration of the product in use. This is the closest an ad in newspapers, magazines, and outdoor and transit advertising can come to showing how a product actually works.

Other Considerations

Although illustrations can be expensive, it is unwise to skimp on costs when purchasing art work or photographs. It is cheaper in the long run to hire a qualified professional than to use less qualified talent, which may result in redoing the job several times.

Sources of photographs can range from stock picture houses and clip art services to museums and newspapers. Art work can be found in these sources, as well as in college and university libraries and art departments. Before using a photograph, be sure to have a model release, which gives permission to use the person or object pictured.

Name _____

Lab _____

Date _____

ASSIGNMENT **9-1.** Using Symbols in Illustrations

Symbols and symbolism are common in human communication, including advertisements. Whether words ("mother") or pictures (American flag), whether graphics (male and female symbols) or ideas ("bankruptcy"), symbolism can conjure up strong images, particularly when used with effective words.

Study the advertisement below and its use of symbolism (the frying pan) to graphically emphasize its point (being burned up by the sun). Then, for the products listed, briefly describe an appropriate visual symbol for each.

1. Aspirin: _____

2. Grass trimmer: _____

3. Savings and loan: _____

Overdone by the sun?

© Plough, Inc. 1974

When the sun burns you up and makes you sizzle. When you're overdone by the sun, stop sunburn pain fast with Solarcaine,® America's number one relief from sunburn pain.

The exclusive Solarcaine formula stops the pain and itching of sunburned skin fast. And while it turns down the heat, it soothes and cools sunburned skin.

So next time you're overdone by the sun, get the heat off your back with Solarcaine. Solarcaine stops sunburn pain and itching fast.

Official Sun Care Products of Florida's Walt Disney World.

Solarcaine
stops sunburn pain–fast.

Source: Courtesy of Schering-Plough Corp.

Chapter 10

Organization

The layout artist must translate the ad concept into visual form. This involves deciding which elements to use in the ad and how to arrange them in the space provided. The first step in this process is the visualization, which is the process of mentally "seeing" the solution to an advertising problem. Thus, visualization is the plan for the ad, and layout is the realization of the plan. There are five major elements to consider when creating a layout: the headline, the illustration, the body copy, the price, and the signature, or logo.

The standard layouts shown in Exhibit 10-1 are designed so that you can simply drop in the elements for your ad. This allows you more time to devote to writing copy, which can't be so easily reduced to a system.

Visualization

The three basic approaches to visualization are (1) showing the product alone, (2) showing it in a setting, and (3) showing it in use. Most other approaches are offshoots from one of these.

Product Alone

In showing the product alone, the emphasis of the visualization is on the product itself. Usually, the product appears to be "suspended in space," with no background, no people, and no props or scenery. This approach is common when the emphasis in the ad is on product design, style, model change, color, beauty, packaging, etc. New product introductions often use this approach to focus attention on the central idea, i.e., the new product. Product selling points are often stressed.

Sometimes, the product is shown by itself to enhance its prestige, implying that it "stands alone." Chanel No. 5 has used this approach for years, showing just the bottle of perfume—without any copy.

Product in a Setting

In this approach, emphasis is on the product in a realistic situation or setting—how it looks in real life. Scenery, props, and other supporting materials may be used to add mood and atmosphere. Focus is broadened from the product to the product as it might actually be seen. The product can be shown in such familiar settings as on a kitchen table, in a den with a roaring fire, or on a businessman's desk. Mood lighting can be used.

Product in Use

The third alternative is to show people actually using the product. This approach emphasizes benefits gained from using the product rather than selling points. Often the setting is simplified so as not to detract from the focus on the product and its use. People should not be shown just standing around or gazing at the product, but actually using the product.

In some cases, the use of the product is implied rather than shown. For example, in a perfume ad showing a woman elegantly attired and seduc-

EXHIBIT **10-1.** Standard Layouts

One-item ads

Two-item ads

Three-item ads

  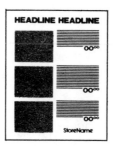  

Source: Newspaper Advertising Bureau

tively posed, the reader assumes that the woman is wearing (i.e., using) the product.

Design

In deciding how to arrange the elements in an ad, the designer must consider both how the ad will look, aesthetically, and how it will work, pragmatically. (For some examples, see Exhibit 10-1.) In designing an attractive and effective ad, you have six basic principles to work with:

1. **Balance.** The condition in which the elements in the ad appear to be "at rest" with themselves. May be formal or informal.

2. **Dominance (also Emphasis).** With several elements (or illustrations), one should be larger than the others. The dominance of one element helps draw attention to the ad.

3. **Flow.** The arrangement of elements to lead the eye through the ad sequentially. Once attention has been drawn to the ad, the reader is directed to other elements in it. Also called "movement" or "direction."

4. **Proportion.** The size relationships of width to height of the ad itself, as well as its elements. The width-height ratio of the "Golden Rectangle" is 2:3. The size of each element should be proportionate to its importance.

5. **Coherence.** The overall visual relationship among the elements in an ad. Every element must cohere or harmonize with all the others. Each should be appropriate for the ad.

6. **Unity.** How well an ad holds together in terms of its total effect. Unity can be accomplished with borders, boxes, overlapping elements, repeating shapes, and background color.

Formats

Once the elements for an ad are selected—and while keeping the basic principles of design in mind—the designer must select a format for the ad. There are as many different arrangements and formats for ads as there are designers. But they tend to fall into some common groupings. The following are some of the more popular layout formats:

1. **Omnibus.** Multiple items are advertised. Commonly used in discount and grocery store ads. Often referred to as a "circus" layout since so much is going on at once. When used for low-priced merchandise (schlock), the layout format is called "schlock."

2. **Picture window.** Features a single, large illustration that dominates the space. Often three-fourths or more of the ad is devoted to illustration. Headline and copy come below the illustration.

3. **Copy-heavy.** As the name implies, this format uses long copy, and all other elements are subordinate to it. Long copy is needed to

EXHIBIT **10-2.** The Thumbnail

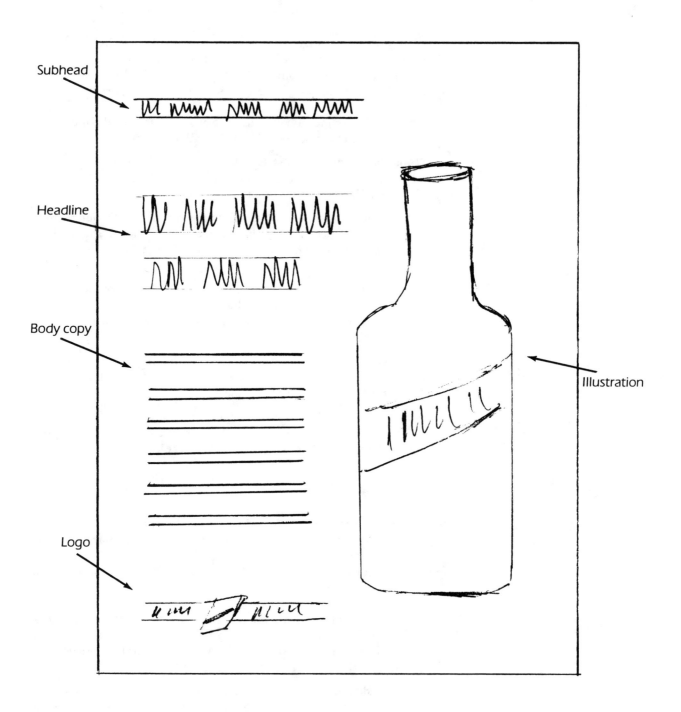

explain a complicated product or service, or to present a detailed selling message.

4. **Multi-panel.** Looks much like a comic strip. This format tells a continuing story in a series of blocks with captions. An actual comic strip may be used, including cartoon characters and balloons with words.

5. **Type-specimen.** The dominant element in the ad is a word or letter set large enough to become the focal point of attention. It might be the logo or a letter used as a symbol or a key word such as "sale."

6. **Alphabet.** Elements in the ad are arranged to resemble some easily recognized letter of the alphabet. Such arrangements are pleasing to the eye, and they help develop flow in the ad.

7. **Mondrian.** Inspired by the Dutch painter Piet Mondrian, this format uses a combination of rectangles (usually illustrations) placed close together. To distinguish it from multi-panel, usually there is no copy between the illustrations, and there is no continuing message from one to the next.

8. **Silhouette.** The illustration includes only foreground figures. Background is omitted.

The "Thumbnail"

If the layout artist decides to use an illustration in the ad, he or she must also decide what it will portray and how large it will be in relation to other elements. Then, the designer must show how all the elements will fit together.

After a general approach and a specific format have been chosen, the layout is presented in the form of a "thumbnail," a rough sketch of what the ad will look like. (See Exhibit 10-2.) The thumbnail provides the layout artist with a visual rendering that will be refined as the layout passes through subsequent stages of clarification.

ASSIGNMENT **10-1.** *Visualizing the Product*

Find one newspaper or magazine ad for each of the three visualization approaches. Look for examples from the same product category (cars, liquor, cosmetics, etc.). Briefly explain why each ad belongs where you have placed it.

1. Product Alone

Product _____

Explanation _____

_____

_____

_____

_____

2. Product in a Setting

Product _____

Explanation _____

_____

_____

_____

_____

3. Product in Use

Product _____

Explanation _____

_____

_____

_____

_____

ASSIGNMENT 10-2. Multiple Visualization for a Product

Visualizing multiple creative solutions for a product or service is a mind-expanding experience. In advertising, it is important to be able to create multiple visualizations with some ease. The three basic ways to visualize a product are a good place to start.

On a separate sheet, make two sketches each for the three basic visualization approaches listed below for a product or service designated by the instructor. For each pair, check the one you think is better.

1. Product Alone
2. Product in Setting
3. Product in Use

Chapter 11

Typography

Ever since Gutenberg invented movable type about 1450, the art of specifying typography for a particular printed piece has grown more complex. Each year new typefaces are introduced. New techniques—primarily dealing with phototypesetting and computers—abound. But in spite of this increasing complexity, numerous basic principles of type selection remain. The following are some which the advertising creative person should heed.

General

1. **Use one typeface throughout.** The use of a single typeface for both text and display type will make the ad more unified and aesthetically pleasing. It will also be less cluttered and less busy. At most, don't use more than two typefaces in one ad.

2. **Use sans serif in display; serif in text.** It is better to use sans serif typefaces in display lines rather than in text. Sans serif is difficult to read in small size. Of course serif faces can be used in display also.

3. **Use captions under pictures.** Always try to use captions and cutlines with pictures. They are read much more often than body copy.

4. **Use normal punctuation.** The purpose of typography is to help communicate a message. This can't be accomplished effectively with unfamiliar and confusing punctuation (such as leaders, multiple exclamation points, etc.).

5. **Use italics sparingly.** Use italics from time to time for emphasis. But do not use them so often that their benefit is lost.

6. **Avoid hard-to-read typefaces.** Although typefaces can set mood and atmosphere, readability and legibility are more important when it comes to communication. Avoid typefaces with heavy swirling strokes, such as Old English, most cursive faces, and many decorative faces.

Headlines

7. **Use down style.** Modern (and normal) style is to set in capital letters only those letters usually capitalized (the first letter of sentences and proper nouns). It is easier to read and looks neater and cleaner.

8. **Avoid all caps.** Any type set in all capital letters is harder to read.

Body Copy (Text)

9. **Set body copy in 10-point minimum.** Anything smaller is too hard to read. Remember many readers wear glasses. Help them.

10. **Break up long copy.** Use frequent paragraphs and subheads.

11. **Set lines 1-1/2 to 2 alphabets wide.** Whatever the type size used, don't set type longer than 1½ to 2 alphabets long (39 to 52 characters).

12. **Don't set body copy in reverse.** Text matter set in reverse is almost always very difficult to read—and might not be read by most people. It is better to mortise a section out of the dark area and set it to be read black on white (or at least on a light background).

13. **Indent paragraphs.** Indented paragraphs increase reading ease since they give the reader a continual starting place. They also work more white space into the type areas, increasing readability.

14. **Use white space between lines.** Rather than set body copy "tight," work in some white space between lines by adding a point or two of leading.

15. **Don't print text over tint blocks.** The most readable copy is black on white. Any other color background reduces readability—the darker, the less readable.

16. **Don't print text over illustrative material.** In so doing, you reduce the readability of the copy because the background interferes with it. Because it may get lost, it may appear to the reader to be relatively unimportant.

17. **Set text matter flush left.** For easier reading, copy blocks should be evenly aligned at the left to give the eye a common starting place. It is permissible to use ragged alignment at the right.

18. **Keep copy areas together.** When there are several copy blocks, it is more convenient for the reader to keep them aligned and close together. Otherwise the entire ad looks cluttered and it is confusing to follow.

19. **Use numerals when listing.** If you are listing several product features or benefits, use numerals instead of bullets or other graphics. Numerals are easier to follow and give added emphasis to copy content.

20. **Avoid "widows" but don't be upset by them.** "Widows" are those very short (often one word) lines that appear at the ends of paragraphs when copy blocks are set. Although one-word lines should be discouraged, they are permissible because they work white space into copy areas. However, never permit widows at the top of a column.

A Guide to Lettering

Neat and professional-looking lettering greatly improves a layout. You need not be a professional letterer, but you should try to become proficient at it.

Several tips should be followed:

- Always use guidelines—very light pencil lines used to keep letters consistent.
- Don't erase them. It wastes time.
- Develop skill with pencil and marker movement. Learn to cover a lot of ground quickly.
- Study the shape and form of various typefaces. Pay attention to how they look. Know the differences among them. "See" them in your mind.
- Build letters from a basic form. Study the step-by-step procedure from the examples in Exhibit 11-1.
- Don't just pass over lettering as something for the artist. Be an active student of lettering. It is important.

EXHIBIT **11-1.** *Building Letters*

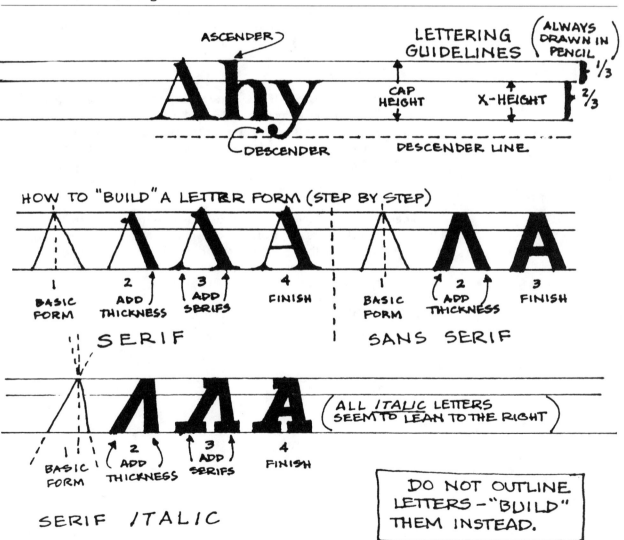

Common Errors in Lettering

You should be aware of several common lettering errors. They are common because most people have never had any instruction in the way letters should be drawn.

The Width Problem

If you are like most people, you will probably draw your letters too thin. Compare them to the letters on the following two pages. There is a type format called "condensed" in which letters are skinny. But don't letter condensed if the type is to be regular. Otherwise the letters won't fit the given space.

The M and W Problem

Most people draw the M and W so that the point in the middle does not touch the bottom or top line. If you look at the two sample typefaces on the following two pages, you'll see that the point goes all the way to the line. This is the way most typefaces are designed. You should sketch these letters accordingly to be accurate.

The Serif Problem

Look at the capital "I." If you draw the small cross lines at the top and bottom, your drawing is incorrect. These lines are called serifs. Either a typeface has serifs or it doesn't. Look at the two typefaces in Exhibit 11-2. One is a sans (without) serif and the other is a serif. You can't mix them (even though most typewriters do).

Other Problems

There are other letters that may cause some confusion. There are several letters for which more than one design is available (and accepted). For instance, the "a" and the "g" have two common styles. Some typefaces offer both as choices to the designer. Either is correct; it's simply a matter of choice. Some typefaces include a curved tail to the "g" and the "q." Others drop the line (called a descender) straight down, with no curve. Again, this is the choice of the designer of the typeface.

EXHIBIT 11-2. Two Typefaces

A Serif Typeface—Times Roman

ABCDEFGHIJKLMNO
PQRSTUVWXYZ
abcdefghijklmnopqrst
uvwxyz
1234567890

A Sans Serif Typeface—Helvetica

ABCDEFGHIJKLMNO
PQRSTUVWXYZ
abcdefghijklmnopqrs
tuvwxyz
1234567890

ASSIGNMENT **11-1.** Hand Lettering

You should become familiar with and proficient in basic hand lettering in order to produce professional-looking layouts. Although most people know how to letter, i.e., print, many of them often do it neither well nor correctly. You do not need to be a professional letterer, but you should be able to letter neatly in the approximate size and style you desire. The neater and more professional-looking your layout is, the more likely it is to receive the attention and consideration it deserves by those evaluating it.

Without any further instruction or reference to any other source, do the following exercises freehand.

A. Complete the alphabet in upper-case letters.
B. Complete the alphabet in lower-case letters.

ASSIGNMENT **11-2.** Transfer Letters

You should gain familiarity and proficiency with transfer letters and masking films.

A. Using transfer letters, set your name in upper and lower case using the guideline below. Pay attention to both word- and letter-spacing. Keep letters straight up and down. Be careful and neat.

B. Using cut-out acetate letters (e.g., Formatt), set your birth month, using the guideline below. Follow the same instructions as above, and be careful in cutting. *Don't* cut directly on the drawing table.

C. Using block-out masking film (e.g., Formopaque), make a large block letter of the grade you expect to receive in this course.

Chapter 12

The Finished Product

Layout Stages

The advertising layout passes through several stages before it gets into print. The complexity of the individual ad usually will determine how many stages are needed. For complex ads, usually five stages are taken from idea to reproduction proof: (1) thumbnail, (2) rough, (3) finished layout, (4) comprehensive, and (5) pasteup. Examples of the thumbnails, rough, and reproduction proof are shown in Exhibits 12-1 to 12-3.

Thumbnail

Designers usually do their early thinking on miniature roughs, called thumbnails. There is no set size, but usually they are 2″ × 3″ or smaller. They are in proportion to the ad as it will finally appear. This doodling stage saves considerable time, while giving necessary tones, outlines, and relationships among the elements. The designer should be able to decide from these which ones have possibilities.

Rough

The next stage is to take the best layout or layouts from thumbnails and produce them in the exact size of the final ad. Although still rough in all aspects, they start to take on the look of real elements, rather than just squiggles, curves and lines. But illustrations still are hastily drawn sketches, headlines are crudely lettered and copy is lined blocks. Often this stage is all that is needed to show the retailer, account, etc.

Finished Layout

This stage is necessary to show clients with less imagination how the final ad might look. A layout selected from the rough stage is now "finished"—headlines are lettered in the style and weight of the final type, illustrations are drawn to look much like the final art, copy is indicated by lines carefully ruled, simulating type. The layout looks much like the final result in all respects.

Comprehensive

When the layout is taken beyond the finished stage it is a comprehensive. It is a perfect facsimile of the final ad. Headlines are carefully lettered

EXHIBIT 12-1. Thumbnails

  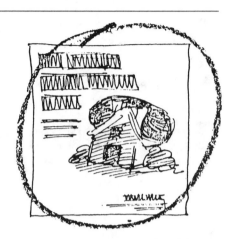

EXHIBIT 12-2. The Rough

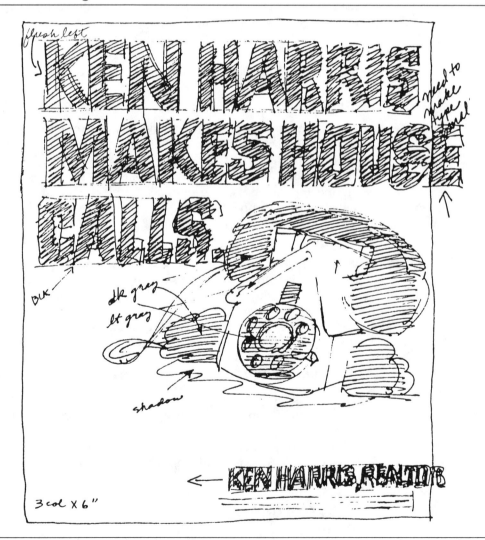

EXHIBIT **12-3.** The Repro

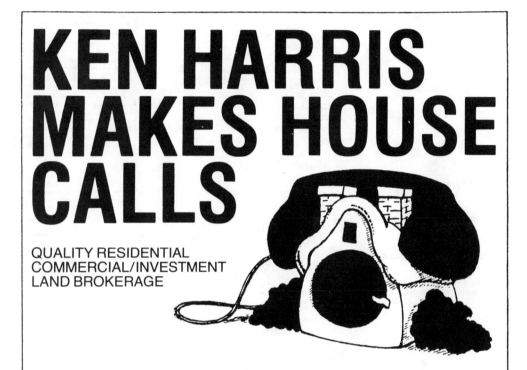

EXHIBIT **12-4.**   Copy Block Lining Examples

Ⓐ SINGLE LINE
Ⓑ DOUBLE LINE
Ⓒ SQUIGGLE
Ⓓ DOUBLE LINE WITH SQUIGGLE (BOLD FACE)
Ⓔ SINGLE BROKEN LINE (EBONY PENCIL)
Ⓕ SINGLE BROKEN LINE (TO INDICATE WORD SPACING)

DO THIS TO INDICATE BOLD FACE WITH LIGHT FACE – DONE TO BREAK UP MONOTONY OF LARGE COPY AREAS

• GUIDELINES SHOULD <u>ALWAYS</u> BE DRAWN LIGHTLY WITH <u>PENCIL</u>

in ink or paint. Art work is close to the final quality. Copy probably will be set and a proof of it pasted in place. Sometimes the comprehensive looks like the final ad itself. The comprehensive is needed primarily for multi-thousand-dollar campaigns in which small errors might be very costly to correct later.

Pasteup

Technically not a layout, the pasteup or mechanical is the production stage necessary to prepare the ad for photographing for plates. All elements of the ad—type, screened photographs, line art, logos, windows for negatives, etc.—are carefully pasted into position for the camera. Usually clients never see pasteups, but some newspapers printed by the offset process do show pasteups (with acetate overlays) as "proofs." Of course, this is dangerous and some form of photocopying should be used.

Reproduction Proof

From the pasteup a print is made, by any of several processes. Two common processes are the Velox and the Photo Mechanical Transfer (PMT). The Velox process is similar to regular photography in that a negative is made from which the print is produced. The PMT does not use a negative but uses a special sensitive paper which is combined with another special paper and sent through a processor. Peeled apart like a Polaroid, the resulting print, if done properly, is difficult to distinguished from the Velox print. For a sample rationale, layout, and repro, see Exhibits 12-5 to 12-7.

Newspaper Layout

The before-and-after ads in Exhibits 12-8 to 12-12 illustrate the importance of design in the layout process. The original ads were created by retailers across the country and appeared in local newspapers. The revised ads were designed by members of the Newspaper Advertising Bureau, Inc., in association with the National Advertising Conference. Each reflects a particular emphasis:

1. **Simplicity.** An ad that is uncluttered and organized will be easier to see in a newspaper.

2. **Sequence.** The two parts here are (a) the focal point—a place for the eye to begin; and (b) flow—positioning each element in a logical place, making the reader's eye to from one element to the next.

3. **Surprise:** This is "creativity": a dramatic, imaginative, or unexpected idea for presenting the information that will make the ad really stand out.

4. **Sell.** This approach emphasizes the benefits and urges the customer to act—buy now!

This checklist should help you take an objective look at the layout to discover any weaknesses. It will also suggest ways to improve any weaknesses you find.

1. **Is there a dominant illustration?** The newspaper reader should be able to tell at a glance what your ad is all about. People read the ads because they're interested in what stores have to sell. A dominant illustration makes it easy for them to do just that.

EXHIBIT **12-5.** *Rationale Sheet*

Marketing Analysis

Who: The prime prospect is male, aged 18–34, including college students, college graduates, and young marrieds in early professional and junior executive positions. Incomes typically are over $20,000. The prospect is an individualist and an innovator. He is adventuresome and sports-minded. He is fashion-conscious but does not just "go along" with new styles if they do not suit him. He buys his own clothes, with his wife's (or girlfriend's) approval.

What: Goudchaux's is a long-established men's clothing store in a fashionable section of a busy shopping area. The store is inviting, with large, well-decorated displays in the windows. It is modern both outside and inside. The merchandise is top quality, with nationally known brands. It is displayed invitingly and conveniently. The store is open at night twice a week, has free parking, offers a free gift-wrapping service, and accepts Visa and MasterCard.

Where: The prospect is brand and store loyal. He returns as long as the service is good. There is only one Goudchaux location, so regular customers know where to find it. Others come by word-of-mouth and advertising.

When: The prospect buys for himself whenever the need arises. Emphasis is on seasonal wardrobe changes and particularly on the autumn "renewal." Gift-giving is a factor in that he influences his lady friend to buy for him at his favorite store, and he buys gifts at the store to give to others.

Why: He enjoys looking good and dressing fashionably. His clothes must fit his lifestyle.

How: Most of his purchases are not on impulse. He usually buys on credit, but just for the convenience. He could afford to pay cash.

Visual Interpretation

The full-page ad in Exhibit 12-7 shows two contemporary males obviously enjoying themselves and pleased with whatever it is they are doing. The figures dominate the ad. They are shown wearing the items featured. Placement of the figures carries the flow from the headline, through the products, to the logo. The left hands of both figures should point toward the logo. The headline attracts attention with a play on words and describes a consumer benefit. Copy is descriptive, yet colorful.

2. **Is the ad suitable for good newspaper reproduction?** Will the illustration and copy print clearly or will they be blurred? Is the illustration style suitable for your newspaper, or should it be changed for better reproduction? One rule: Never run body copy in reverse or surprinted over a halftone.

3. **Does the ad have a distinctive, recognizable format?** Would your readers, especially the store's regular customers, recognize the ad even without the store name? Instant recognition is important, and this is particularly true for the store's small-space ads.

4. **Does the ad have a recognizable logo?** The logo should include the store's name, address and telephone number. It is also important to include other pertinent information, such as store hours, credit information, etc., and these should be seen in every ad.

EXHIBIT **12-6.** Sample Rough Newspaper Layout

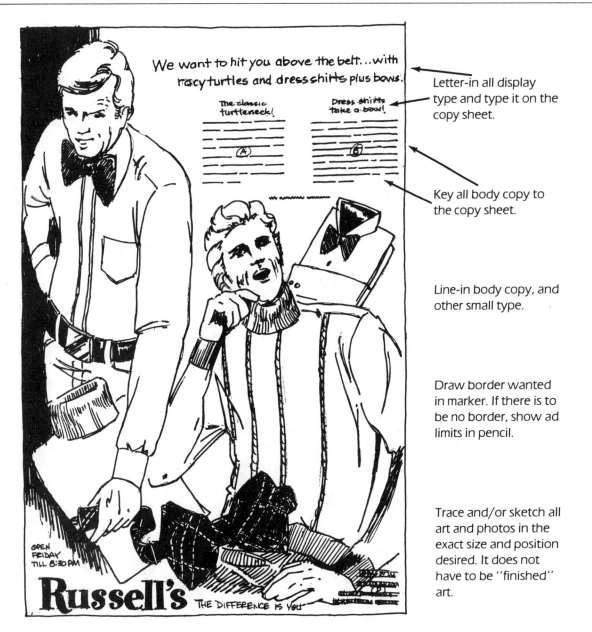

We want to hit you above the belt...with racy turtles and dress shirts plus bows.

The classic turtleneck!

Dress shirts take a bow!

Ⓐ

Ⓑ

OPEN FRIDAY TILL 8:30 PM

Russell's THE DIFFERENCE IS YOU

Letter-in all display type and type it on the copy sheet.

Key all body copy to the copy sheet.

Line-in body copy, and other small type.

Draw border wanted in marker. If there is to be no border, show ad limits in pencil.

Trace and/or sketch all art and photos in the exact size and position desired. It does not have to be "finished" art.

5. **Is the ad well organized and easy to follow?** A poorly organized layout makes things difficult for the reader. This is especially true for ads with many items of merchandise, where a well-organized layout with a headline that applies to all the items adds up to an inviting presentation of the merchandise.

6. **Does the ad have a clean, uncluttered look?** Many people's first impression of a store is from its advertising. Does the ad make a good impression, and is the merchandise in the ad easy to find? Readers are easily discouraged.

EXHIBIT **12-7.** Ad as Run

7. **Is more white space needed?** White space is probably the most underestimated element in newspaper advertising. Solid masses without any breathing space are usually unattractive. Consider using more white space; it pays off in attention value.

8. **Does the illustration demonstrate a benefit or show the merchandise in use?** This helps the reader visualize herself or himself using the product, and this may be an important step toward making the sale. Apparel ads are usually more effective when they show the merchandise being worn.

EXHIBIT **12-8.** Simplicity

The original ad is attractive and well-balanced, but the revision is easier for the reader to follow and conveys a stronger fashion image simply by aligning the elements horizontally and vertically.

Original

Revision

Source: Newspaper Advertising Bureau, Inc.

9. **Is the illustration large enough?** Research shows that ads with large merchandise pictures get higher readership than ads with small illustrations or with no illustration. People want to see the merchandise you're selling.

EXHIBIT **12-9.** Sequence

Good use of white space is only a part of making an ad appealing, as illustrated by the original. The revision enlarges one figure to give the ad a focal point that will attract attention and pull the other elements together.

Original

Revision

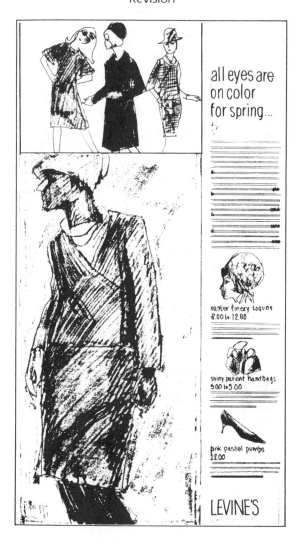

Source: Newspaper Advertising Bureau, Inc.

The TV Storyboard

When you think of the development and product of television commercials, you do not ordinarily think of "layout" playing a role. But it does, and an important role, at that.

The layout in television is the storyboard: a script with pictures, which

EXHIBIT **12-10.** Sequence

Although both ads have clean, attractive illustrations and the same number of copy blocks, the revision has an "S" flow, allowing the eye to move easily and naturally from one item to the next.

Original   Revision

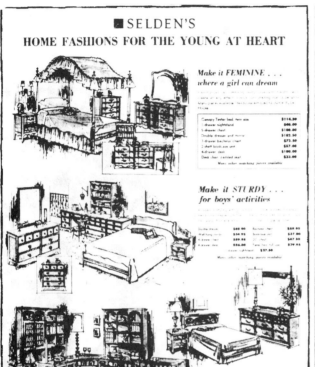

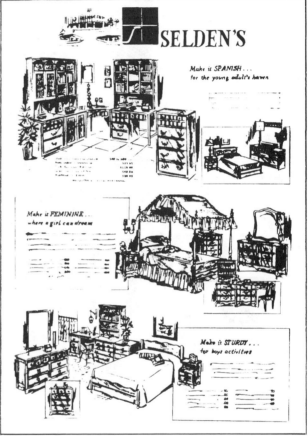

Source: Newspaper Advertising Bureau, Inc.

is the artist's rendering of each scene as it will ultimately be seen on the screen. (See Exhibits 12-13 and 12-14.) The pictures on the storyboard may tell the story of the commercial even better, and certainly more graphically, than do the words.

The storyboard is important because it is the vital bridge when the ad agency presents the concept to the client. A script can be read quite differently by two different people. It may seem perfectly clear to the agency writer and to the account people. But it may not be as clear to the client. The advantage of the storyboard is that it cannot be misunderstood; it actually "shows" the commercial, scene by scene.

EXHIBIT **12-11.** Surprise

This example shows how a good small ad can become a great small ad. The revision reduces the number of elements and adds contrast for big impact.

Original   Revision

Source: Newspaper Advertising Bureau, Inc.

The storyboard is the method used most frequently by agencies in presentations to the client. It serves to "visualize" the script—easily and quickly.

It is also valuable to the production house assigned by the agency to shoot the commercial. It is used as a guide because it indicates, with clarity and specificity, precisely what the agency writer and art director have in mind. It represents the thinking of all the creative people involved.

EXHIBIT **12-12.** Sell

In the original ad, the headline competes with the other elements for attention. In the revision, it is given the prominence due a once-in-a-great-while merchandising event.

Original

Revision

Source: Newspaper Advertising Bureau, Inc.

EXHIBIT **12-13.** Storyboard: Drawing

1. CUST: Which one of you guys is Murph?
BOTH: I am. (CHUCKLE)
MURPH: My son.
JR.: My dad.
MAN APPROACHES MURPH AND JR. AT PUMPS

2. CUST: Fella told me to see a guy named
Murph about an unleaded regular to stop my
knocking and pinging.
SR.: Right!
CUST: (TO SR.) But my car's knocking on
unleaded regular already!

3. JR.: Then use 76 unleaded regular.
CUST: (TO JR.) Why?

4. SR.: It's a higher octane unleaded
regular. 89 compared to 87 in many others.
So it's got more spirit.
CUST: (TO SR.) A higher octane unleaded?
MURPH POINTS TO PUMP

5. CUST: (TO JR.) Sounds good to me!
(TO SR.) So...which Murph do I see to fill
up my car?
MAN IS CONFUSED.

6. BOTH: (POINT TO EACH OTHER) Him!
(CHUCKLE)

7. FILL 'ER UP...
STANDARD CLOSE

8. WITH SPIRIT

9. JR.: The 89 octane unleaded with more
spirit!
SR.: Allow me! (TAKES NOZZLE)
SONG: THE SPIRIT OF 76
MORTICE MURPH AND JR.

10. THE SPIRIT OF 76.
SUPER: The Spirit of 76

SOURCE: Courtesy of Union Oil Company of California.

EXHIBIT **12-14.** Storyboard: Photo

1. CUST: Which one of you guys is Murph?
BOTH: I am.

2. MURPH: My son.
JR.: My dad.

3. CUST: Fella told me to see a Murph about an unleaded regular to help stop my knocks and my pinging.

4. SR: That's right!
JR: He's right!

5. CUST: Yeah, but my car's knocking on unleaded regular already.

6. JR: Then use Seventy-Six unleaded regular.

7. SR: It's not like ordinary unleaded regulars.

8. SR: It's got more spirit.
CUST: More spirit?
JR: Right.

9. Which Murph do I see to fill up my car?

10. BOTH: Him!

11. SONG: FILL 'ER UP WITH SPIRIT.
JR: Try a better unleaded regular.
SR: Allow me.

12. SONG: THE SPIRIT OF SEVENTY-SIX.

SOURCE: Courtesy of Union Oil Company of California.

ASSIGNMENT **12-1.** Copy Block Lining

Body copy is never typed or written on the layout. Only headlines, subheadlines, and other display type are actually lettered on the layout. Body copy is lined. It is important when creating layouts to represent elements as closely as possible to the way they will look in final form, so the lining should look professional as well as simulate type.

There are several methods of lining copy blocks, each with its advantages and disadvantages. Some common methods are shown in Exhibit 12-4. Practice them all until you can do them well and quickly. Then use the one you can do the best, the most neatly, and the most professionally. Modern practice suggests using felt-tip markers, but pencils may also be used.

Use a T-square for the most attractive lining. Always use light side guidelines, and *don't erase them.* Side guidelines help the production people measure the width, as well as give the eye limits.

Practice all the lining methods below, first with a T-square and then freehand. Practice until you can do them all quickly and well.

ASSIGNMENT **12-2.** Doing the Layout

Do the layout for three advertisements, using current campaigns as models. For a sample print layout, see Exhibit 12-6.

1. Go through any recent copies of any popular magazines you are familiar with and select ads from three campaigns that (a) impress you as being well done, and (b) contain the kind of pictorial treatment you feel best qualified to do.

2. You will observe that in an effective ad the basic message is crystallized in the illustration. For this assignment, choose ads that use art work rather than actual photographs.

3. Before you start doing the layout, you should have clearly in mind how your ad is going to look. Write a brief, clear description, 20 to 25 words, of the pictorial treatment you propose. Also, prepare a rough layout, full size, for your own guidance.

4. Now prepare the layout, in comprehensive form, for each of the campaigns, carrying the same sales story and the same general format used in the original.

5. When you present your completed assignment, be sure to include tear sheets (at least one typical ad) from each of the campaigns you have used as models.

Part A

Assume that your client is Penguin Raceway, a successful enterprise which features harness racing and is located on the outskirts of a midwestern city. The track has just been purchased by an aggressive, promotion-minded owner who feels that while attendance has been good, it can be better with effective promotion on radio and TV.

His goal is to attract a more diversified patronage, including reputable and cultured people in the upper-middle-income bracket, as well as women and married couples.

He feels the way to accomplish this is to play up the aesthetic aspects of the track: the beauty of the plant, the luxury and decoration of the restaurants and public areas, the attractiveness of the landscaping, and the vivid beauty of the horses.

Additional attractions: excellent dining, convenient parking and betting facilities, fine quality horses, and famous jockeys. Other features: easy accessibility from the city, courteous attendants and window clerks. Also, a new, free bus service from the parking lot to the stands. All in all, this is a track designed for the patron's total comfort and enjoyment.

Do the storyboard for a 60-second TV commercial aimed at the audience described above, promoting Penguin Raceway as a socially acceptable and respectable place to visit. Trace the blanks provided below to your own layout paper; use at least 9 frames for your storyboard.

Part B

Do the storyboard for a 30-second spin-off of the commercial done in Assignment 12-3. Music and sound effects may be used. Trace the blanks below onto your own layout paper.

PART IV
Print Media

Chapter 13

Newspapers

Introduction

Through the years, even though various new media have been introduced, newspaper advertising has not only survived but continues to reign as the advertising medium that annually collects the largest volume of advertising dollars from local, regional, and national advertisers.

Most of a newspaper's income comes from its advertising revenue, which pays for 70 percent of its production costs. The result is a vast profusion of ads that infringe on the editorial matter—in some local papers almost to the point of extinguishing it. However, newspaper readers don't seem to mind. In fact, nearly everyone is accustomed to inspecting the ads for good values.

The problem is that with all these ads, there is considerable competition to get the prospective buyer's eye and hold his attention. It's not enough to feature a good product or a bona fide sale; the manner in which the item or event is presented will determine the success or failure of the ad. This vital job of outshining the competition falls to the layout artist and copywriter. They must produce an ad with originality, freshness, and distinction.

Advantages

Perhaps the outstanding advantage of newspaper advertising is its credibility. Most television, radio, and magazine advertising is presented in a medium devoted primarily to entertainment. People tend to believe what they read in newspapers because the medium is mainly a vehicle for objectively reported news.

Other advantages of newspaper advertising include good reach and frequency, flexibility, and convenience.

Reach and Frequency

Newspapers reach a majority of households in most markets. And they do so at a relatively low cost. In addition, they are passed on from reader to reader, thus gaining maximum penetration. Unlike magazines, newspapers are published daily or weekly and thereby provide advertisers with an opportunity to repeat their advertising messages frequently over a short span of time.

Flexibility

Newspaper advertisements are flexible in that they can present any number of items and can use either black and white or color. Ads can be changed quickly, in response to sudden alterations in product availability, marketing plans, or consumer demands. Newspaper ads also provide good retail tie-in possibilities. They can range in size from one inch to full and even multiple pages.

Convenience

Newspapers can be carried everywhere and read at any time or place: on commuter trains, in business offices, at beauty parlors, and in living rooms. They can be left behind by original purchasers and picked up by new readers. Ads can be clipped and saved—for study, comparison, or later use at the reader's convenience.

Guidelines

The problem is that many newspaper ads fail to exploit these advantages, and many show no creative skill. In fact, many of them are poorly done. This means that they stand a good chance of not being noticed, of getting lost in the crowd. Usually, newspaper ads are ineffective, especially at the local level, because they are composed by people with little or no advertising experience or expertise. Such people might benefit from the following suggestions for copy and layout. If adhered to, and infused with a small spark of creativity, these guidelines can increase readership and move merchandise.

1. **Make your ads easily recognizable.** Advertisements that are distinctive in their use of art, layout techniques, and typefaces usually enjoy higher readership than run-of-the-mill advertising does. Make your ads distinctively different from the advertising of your competitors. Then keep the appearance consistent so that readers will recognize your ads even before they read them.

2. **Use a simple layout.** The layout should carry the reader's eye through the message easily and in proper sequence: from headline to illustration to explanatory copy to price to store name or logo. Avoid the use of too many different typefaces, overly decorative borders, and reverses. These devices are distracting and reduce the number of readers who receive your entire message.

3. **Use a dominant element.** A large picture or headline helps insure quick visibility. Photographs and realistic drawings have about equal attention-getting value, but photographs of real people win more readership. So do action pictures. Photographs of local people or places also have high attention value. Use good art work. It pays off in extra readership.

4. **Use a prominent benefit headline.** The reader asks of any ad, "What's in it for me?" Don't hide the answer. Select the main benefit and feature it in a compelling headline. "How to" headlines encourage readership, as do headlines with specific information or

helpful suggestions. Headlines are easier to read if they're black-on-white and not printed over part of an illustration.

5. **Let your white space work for you.** Don't overcrowd the ad. White space is an important layout element. White space focuses the reader's attention on your ad and makes headline and illustration stand out. When a crowded ad is necessary, e.g., for a sale on many items, group the items so that the reader can find his way through them easily.

6. **Make your copy interesting and readable.** Copy should be enthusiastic and sincere, but not exaggerative. A block of copy written in complete sentences is easier to read than one composed of phrases and random words. In designing the layout of a copy block, consider a boldface lead-in. Small pictures in sequence will often help readership. Don't be too clever, and avoid unusual or difficult words.

7. **State price or range of prices.** Don't be afraid to quote your price. That's what retail advertising is all about. Readers often overestimate omitted prices. If the advertised price is high, explain why the item represents a good value—perhaps because of superior materials or workmanship, or extra features. If the price is low, support it with factual statements which create belief, such as information on a close-out sale, a special purchase, or a clearance.

8. **Specify branded merchandise.** If the item is a known brand, say so in your advertising. Manufacturers spend large sums to sell their goods, and you can capitalize on their advertising while enhancing the reputation of your store by featuring branded items. Using the brand name may also qualify the ad for cooperative advertising allowances from the manufacturer.

9. **Include related items.** Make two sales instead of one by offering related items along with the featured one. For instance, when a dishwasher is advertised, also show a disposal. If you're advertising a dress or suit you can increase potential sales by also including shoes, hats, or handbags in the same ad.

10. **Feature the main fact.** First, obtain all the facts the customer may wish to know about the advertised merchandise. Then select the one fact or idea of greatest interest to the largest number of prospective customers. The product feature should be different from and, hopefully, superior to that of similar products. Once it has been determined, it is this quality that should be emphasized or dramatized.

11. **Include all important information.** It is truly amazing that so many retail ads are printed in newspapers without vital information. Besides store identification and price, other important facts to consider include address, telephone number, hours open, free parking, and such services as delivery, gift wrapping, layaway, and credit plans including credit cards accepted. To include everything might make the ad too cumbersome, but at least the most important facts should be given.

12. **Urge your readers to buy now.** Ask for the sale. You can stimulate prompt action by using such phrases as "limited supply" or "this week only." If mail order coupons are included in the ad, provide

spaces large enough for customers to fill them in easily. Don't generalize. Be specific at all times.

Preparation of Print Advertisements

Print advertisements include those for newspapers, magazines, and business publications. These are instructions of how to prepare materials to turn in during this class. Be aware that each ad department, agency, medium, or other firm will have its own way to prepare materials. Do it their way.

Most major assignments in this section will consist of three basic pieces: a copy sheet, a layout, and a rationale sheet. Always put your name and lab section in the upper right corner of every page. Identify the advertiser and the medium at upper left.

Copy Sheet

All copy should be submitted on a separate sheet of 8½″ × 11″ typing paper. (See Exhibit 13-1.) Do not use notebook or ruled paper (unless assigned as an in-lab exercise). Always type and double space all copy. Type everything from the layout sheet onto the copy sheet, including headlines, subheadlines and other display lines.

If there is more than one continuous copy area, designate each copy block on the layout with a letter, which corresponds to a designated piece of copy on the copy sheet. This is called "keying the copy" Study and follow the sample copy sheet. Copy sheets should be "clean," that is, with no mistakes, misspellings, etc. Be very careful to make sure copy sheets and layouts agree in every detail.

Layouts

Layouts for print ads are done on visualizing or tracing paper. Do not draw layouts directly to the edge of the paper; leave some white space all around. Do not paste anything on the layout. Only trace or do original sketches. The layout is a blueprint, so everything shown should be in the exact position and size you want. Your layout usually will be a "rough."

Letter on the layout all display copy (larger than what is normally called "body copy"). This includes headlines, subheadlines, dominant prices, slogans and logos. Always use light guidelines (pencil) when lettering, and do not erase them.

Body copy is designated on the layout by one of several lining methods. Use guidelines to show width and do not erase them. Make copy areas correspond to the copy sheet by placing a small letter in the center of the copy block (in pencil) and circle it. Line copy blocks in fine-tipped felt marker.

Rationale

Provide reasons and explanations for what you do in a rationale. This will help you develop your creative thinking and help you develop the advertising strategy or concept.

EXHIBIT **13-1.** Sample Copy Sheet

Goudchaux's
Baton Rouge Gazette
Full page
Black and white

HEADLINE: We want to hit you above the belt . . . with racy turtles and dress shirts plus bows!

SUBHEAD: The classic turtleneck!

COPY A: Turtlenecks are the most versatile, comfortable, and good-looking sport look we've seen. Wear them with slacks or jeans . . . add a sport coat for a spiffier look. Goudchaux's has turtlenecks in flat and ribbed knits from names like Puritan, McGregor, and Jantzen. They come in polyester, polyester blends, and cotton knits. Sizes S, M, L, XL. $9.00 to $20.00.

SUBHEAD: Dress shirts take a bow!

COPY B: What a match! Good-looking shirts in classy patterns look even better when you add just the right bow tie. Goudchaux's has long sleeve dress shirts in polyester knits and polyester/cotton blends from Sero, Enro, Arrow, Van Heusen, and more famous names. Sizes 14½ to 17 in up to 35" sleeves. $9.00 to $16.00. Snazzy bow ties come in clip-ons, banded and tie-your-own styles. Goudchaux's has polyester blend ties by Wembley, Don Loper and Beau Brummel. $4.50 to $6.00.

SUBHEAD: Goudchaux's Men's Store, West Wing

COPY C: OPEN FRIDAY TILL 8:30 P.M.

LOGO: Goudchaux's

SLOGAN: THE DIFFERENCE IS *YOU!*

COPY D: GOUDCHAUX'S, 1500 Main . . . where you never pay interest or finance charges. Phone 348-1192. Shop 9:00 to 5:45 daily. Monday and Thursday nights to 8:30.

\#   \#   \#

EXHIBIT **13-2.** Newspaper Checklist and Evaluation

	Very Good	Good	Fair	Weak	Very Weak
RATIONALE:					
1. Prospect analysis	[ ]	[ ]	[ ]	[ ]	[ ]
2. Advertisement analysis	[ ]	[ ]	[ ]	[ ]	[ ]
LAYOUT:					
1. Dominant illustration or element	[ ]	[ ]	[ ]	[ ]	[ ]
2. Use of white space	[ ]	[ ]	[ ]	[ ]	[ ]
3. Ad recognizable, distinctive	[ ]	[ ]	[ ]	[ ]	[ ]
4. Simple layout	[ ]	[ ]	[ ]	[ ]	[ ]
HEADLINE:					
1. Prominent benefit headline	[ ]	[ ]	[ ]	[ ]	[ ]
2. Store name in headline	[ ]	[ ]	[ ]	[ ]	[ ]
COPY:					
1. Copy interesting and readable	[ ]	[ ]	[ ]	[ ]	[ ]
2. Prices featured prominently	[ ]	[ ]	[ ]	[ ]	[ ]
3. Name brands specified	[ ]	[ ]	[ ]	[ ]	[ ]
4. Related items included	[ ]	[ ]	[ ]	[ ]	[ ]
5. Action urged	[ ]	[ ]	[ ]	[ ]	[ ]
6. Copy complete (store information)	[ ]	[ ]	[ ]	[ ]	[ ]
MISCELLANEOUS:					
1. Mechanics					
A. Lettering	[ ]	[ ]	[ ]	[ ]	[ ]
B. Sketching/tracing	[ ]	[ ]	[ ]	[ ]	[ ]
C. Copy blocks lined and keyed	[ ]	[ ]	[ ]	[ ]	[ ]
2. Overall idea and ad	[ ]	[ ]	[ ]	[ ]	[ ]
3. Spelling and grammar	[ ]	[ ]	[ ]	[ ]	[ ]
4. Followed directions (on time, etc.)	[ ]	[ ]	[ ]	[ ]	[ ]

COMMENTS:

EXHIBIT **13-3.** Newspaper Ads

These prize-winning ads demonstrate the variety of styles and formats that newspapers can accommodate. The photo used in the Harris & Friends ads speaks for itself and requires little copy. The JP Audio ad makes its point forcefully by inviting reader participation. And the Higbee's ad is remarkable for conveying no information at all about the company's product.

SOURCE: Reprinted from *Creative Newspaper '79*, Newspaper Advertising Bureau, Inc.

EXHIBIT **13-3.** Newspaper Ads (continued)

The Fiat ad combines the best of two worlds: good illustration and relevant copy, both of which focus on such product features as style, comfort, and dependability. The Witts ad cleverly adapts the multi-item format to the requirements of a 30-day sale. Zeidler & Zeidler sent Season's Greetings to its customers with a striking illustration that communicates style and sophistication.

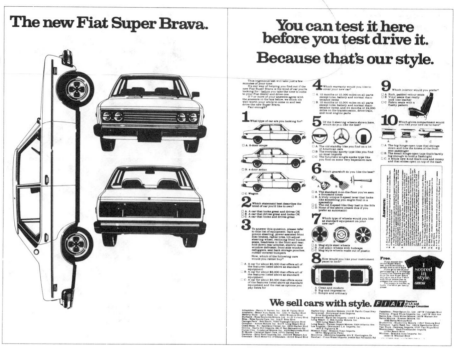

SOURCE: Reprinted from *Creative Newspaper '79*, Newspaper Advertising Bureau, Inc.

ASSIGNMENT 13-1. Writing a Newspaper Ad

You are the copywriter for a large department store. The manager of the men's clothing department gives you the fact sheet shown below, from which you are to write the copy for a half-page ad. This ad will appear in the local paper of a medium-size midwestern city.

Sterling Men's Fashions

Features a special combination outfit from Haggar:

1. Smartly styled, solid color business suit.
2. Extra pair of contrasting check trousers.
3. Two belts, one for suit, one for slacks.
4. Dress shirt.
5. Sport shirt.

May be worn as five great outfits:

1. Full suit.
2. Suit coat and contrasting slacks with dress shirt.
3. Suit coat and slacks with sport shirt.
4. Sport shirt (Arrow) with suit pants.
5. Sport shirt (Arrow) with sport slacks.

Selling Points:

1. 100% Dacron polyester is wrinkle resistant.
2. Suit tailored with self-stitching on lapels and flap pockets.
3. Colors: navy, chocolate, camel.
4. Sizes: 38 to 46.
5. Price: Only $185 ($225 if purchased separately).

Store Points:

1. Two locations: Downtown and Mission Mall.
2. Parking: Two hours free downtown; free at mall.
3. Hours: 9:30 A.M. to 5:30 P.M. Monday through Saturday. Open until 9:00 P.M. Thursdays.
4. Telephone: 456-7890.
5. Charge: Accepts Visa and MasterCard and has own charge plan.
6. Free gift wrapping and delivery.
7. Has complete line of men's furnishings, from underwear and shoes to accessories and a formal wear department. Carries name brands.

ASSIGNMENT 13-2. Writing a Newspaper Ad

You are the copywriter assigned by the ad agency to the Peoples Bank account. Write the copy for a half-page newspaper ad, incorporating the specific strategy outlined by the bank's president.

The president of Peoples Bank, located in a medium-size midwestern city, is dissatisfied with its rate of growth. The bank had only a 10 percent increase in the past five years, well below that of competitive banks. In a meeting with his advertising agency, the president expresses the opinion that while it is important to build prestige, he does not believe that a campaign that stresses institutional advertising will increase total deposits.

He believes that the agency's campaign for the forthcoming year should be more specific and concrete in the benefits it offers its customers. The campaign should include the fact that Peoples Bank gives individualized service to all its patrons, big or small, and should feature such benefits as "no charge on checking accounts if you maintain a balance of $200, with full interest paid on the balance." He also tells the agency principals that it is important to build a stronger position against savings and loan corporations paying higher interest rates. The way to combat this, he says, is to have his advertising emphasize that "There's no substitute for a bank savings account."

ASSIGNMENT 13-3. Writing a Newspaper Ad

Based on the information provided below, write a strong promotional newspaper ad, which announces a special purchase sale, two days only—Wednesday and Thursday, September 17 and 18.

A well-known men's store in Boston, Massachusetts, has made a special purchase of 5,000 high-quality white shirts. Because the manufacturer is a national advertiser, the brand name is not mentioned, and the store label has been substituted.

The shirts are standard styles: broadcloth and Oxford cloth, with button-down collars, in a full range of sizes, some with French cuffs.

The single unit price is $11.95, which the buyer says is about two dollars under the nationally advertised price. The shirts may be purchased singly, or three for $33.50. These are the kinds of shirts men will want to stock up on.

While this ad is primarily promotional, it should also carry strong institutional aspects: free parking, layaway plan, the store's long history of quality products, etc.

ASSIGNMENT **13-4.** Writing a Newspaper Ad

You are the copywriter for the Amana Refrigeration, Inc. You are given the fact sheet shown below, from which you are to write the copy for a full-page ad to appear in newspapers throughout the country.

Amana Touchmatic Radarange® Microwave Oven

Cooking as Simple as 1-2-3:

1. Take food directly from freezer and put it in Amana Touchmatic Radarange. Can stay on china, ovenwear, paper plates, plasticwear, etc.
2. Simply touch numbers for defrost time. Touch defrost. Touch numbers for cooking time. Touch start. With a "memory" feature, it remembers each of these, including when to shut itself off and call it to your attention with a "beep."
3. Ready to serve dinner.

Features:

1. See-through door.
2. Stainless steel interior.
3. Roomy inside, large enough for family-size turkey.
4. Removable glass tray to catch spatters and spills.
5. 700 watts of cooking power.
6. Slo Cook simmers food.
7. 10-year limited warranty on major components.

Benefits:

1. Cooks almost everything in one-fourth the usual time.
2. Set and forget, to attend to other activities.
3. Operates on ordinary 120v household current.
4. Slo Cook brings out all the full, rich flavors like a slow oven, in much less time.
5. Food gets hot but oven stays cool so cleanup is a snap.

Slogan:

"If it doesn't say Amana—
it's not a Radarange."

Amana Refrigeration, Inc.
Amana, Iowa 52204

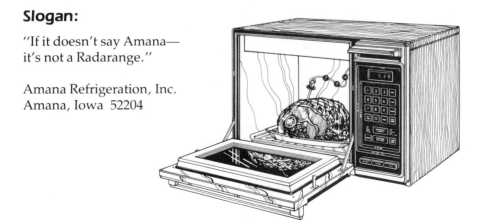

SOURCE: Courtesy of Amana Refrigeration, Inc./Amana, Iowa 52204

Chapter 14

Classified

Classified advertising has been around a long time. In fact, a classified ad appeared more than two centuries ago when *The Virginia Gazette,* on July 20, 1776, ran an ad headed "Seamen Wanted."

History does not disclose how many venturesome young men responded, but we do know that more than $14.6 billion was spent on classified in 1981.

The classified section of the newspaper is sometimes referred to as "the people's marketplace." It is where the average person can buy on a word or line basis. Classified advertising requires no knowledge of typography, layout, or illustration. It does, however, require some basic writing skills and adherence to a few simple guidelines.

Classified ads need not entertain the reader. Their function is to inform. And the information should be conveyed without gratuitous embellishment. The writing should be simple and clear. It should present an orderly listing of the vital facts. And it should be done succinctly.

After all, the reader must understand what the advertiser is saying or he will not respond. Lack of comprehension in classified advertising is often due to abbreviation and the use of uncommon words. When that happens, the reader may fail to understand the ad and a potential sale will be lost.

What essentials should be listed in an effective classified ad? A good way to answer this is to put yourself in the reader's place. If you were reading the ad, what would you want to know about the item advertised? Shown in Exhibit 14-1 is a sample of the type of reminder cards that copywriters can use.

EXHIBIT **14-1.** Reminder Card

Remind Your Advertisers of These Copy Essentials

These are the points that ads should cover to achieve best results:

AUTOS FOR SALE
Make
Year
Body style
Motor (V8? Horsepower?)
Transmission
Power equipment
Finish
Mileage
Previous use (one owner?)
Mechanical condition
Accessories
Tires, battery
Interior
Price, terms, down payment

HELP WANTED
Kind of job
Hours
Security
Benefits
Facilities
Vacation
Privileges
Advancement opportunity
Wages
Experience necessary
Age preferred
Qualifications
Location
How to apply

FARM ITEMS
What is item
Make (brand name)
Model
Year
Condition
Overhauled
Attachments
Hours of previous use
Paint
Price

RENTALS
Location
Number of rooms
Closets
Bath, shower
Garage
Heating
Air conditioning
Furnishings
Utilities furnished
Elevator
Neighborhood
Convenience to stores,
    schools, and transportation
Children accepted
Pets allowed
Privileges—phone, kitchen
    laundry, television, etc.
When available
Price

BUSINESS SERVICES
Kind of service
Experience
Special equipment
Trained personnel
Guarantee
Availability
Follow-up services
Hours
Insured? Bonded?
Prices

LIVESTOCK AND PETS
Kind of animal
Breed
Age
Size or weight
Color, markings
Registered
Price

MERCHANDISE AND
MISCELLANEOUS
FOR SALE
What is item?
Brand name
Size
Age
Color
Condition
Specifications
Previous usage
Upholstery
Finish
Accessories and attachments
Hours to see offering
Price

REAL ESTATE FOR SALE
Location
Construction (frame? brick?)
Architecture, landscaping
Number of rooms, description
Number of bedrooms
Condition, age
Possession date
Convenience to stores, schools, and
    transportation
Lot size, zoning
Garage
Bathrooms
Kitchen (disposal?)
Basement, recreation room
City sewer, utilities
Heating
Fireplace
Plumbing
Built-ins, closets
Features for children
Price, terms, how much down?

ASSIGNMENT **14-1.** Writing Your Own Classified Ads

Much can be learned from studying and writing classified ads. Most classified ads reduce the product or service to its most basic selling points and/or benefits. However, often the most effective ones are those that add meat to the skeleton, putting some "sell" to the bare facts.

Write classified ads for the following subjects. Provide the specific facts and supporting information. Remember that in classified every additional line costs more money, and just one unnecessary word may mean an additional line. Make every word count. At the same time, one additional effective word might stimulate action.

A. Write classified ads for the following, for your campus newspaper:
1. Seeking transportation to Nashville for a Dolly Parton concert
2. Locating a roommate for yourself
3. Selling your 1975 Volkswagen Superbeetle
4. Selling four used textbooks
5. Selling your stereo record player
6. Locating tickets to the upcoming Cotton Bowl game in Dallas

B. Write classified ads for the following, for your local city newspaper:
1. Seeking your lost Collie
2. Selling an old upright piano
3. Having a garage sale
4. Selling a swing set
5. Offering guitar lessons
6. Looking for a job

ASSIGNMENT **14-2.** Writing Classified Ads for Others

You are employed in the classified ad department of a local newspaper. A woman gives you the following information about her house, which is for sale. The amount of money she wishes to spend on the ad entitles her to 35 words, plus a headline. You write the ad for her.

This is the information she gives you:

The house, colonial in style, is located in the country club section. It is 12 years old and has 8 rooms, including kitchen, den, dining room, living room, playroom, and three bedrooms. It also has two full baths, one with stall shower. The house is in excellent condition throughout. It is on ½ acre of ground, which is fully landscaped. The yearly taxes are $1,210. The house, which is made of brick and white clapboard, is priced at $102,000. The price is firm. Appliances include: dishwasher, dryer, washer, refrigerator, and disposal. It is centrally air conditioned. A new fence encircles the property, and a new play gym is in the back yard. The house is just two blocks from a complete shopping area, and it is in close proximity to elementary and high schools, as well as to churches of all denominations.

Note: Headline no longer than 5 words.

ASSIGNMENT **14-3.** ·Copy Condensation

On occasion, because of space limitations and sometimes for clarity and style, copy must be condensed. Unnecessary words should be eliminated. Vital words that help "sell" should be left or added. Word order is important, also. Sometimes words must be rearranged for more logical and persuasive presentation.

Condense the following letter, sent to your local newspaper's classified department, into an effective classified ad. You may use this page as a worksheet. Then, type the finished ad to be turned in.

Sept 10, 1983

Dear classified dept.

I have me some odds and ends I wanna sell next Fre. and Sat. in my garage. This stuff have ben siting around here and I could use the money. First off, theres a riding mower and other yard and lawn tools. And I have a skil saw and a drill and some other shop tools I don't use no more. Then theres two bikes, a trike and a little wagon which needs painting some. I also have some clothes which still have some wear left, such as some shirts and pants and a good 3 piece suit. Oh yes, my wife wants to get rid of our old washing machine and one of those outside line drying things. She too has a bunch of plants, some antique glasses and jars, some dresses and shoes and a roll top desk. We live in Cedarville at 1315 Wonder road.

Thank you,

Tim Wallace

341-2761

ASSIGNMENT **14-4.** Copy Condensation

Condense the following letter, sent to your local newspaper's classified department, into an effective classified ad. You may use this page as a worksheet. Then, type the finished ad to be turned in.

2711 East Oak Dr.
Plankton, Ohio

Dear Sirs:

I want to run a classified ad in your paper this Sunday. If I get some calls but don't sell it, I'll run it again later. Put it under the "stereo" section. Here are the details that you can use to write the ad.

What I have to sell is a stereo that has everything on it. I want to see it because I need money to pay for my tuition and don't have enough money. It is a SuperSound SMS-1016 Quadraphase setero with components. It is a compact system which includes AM and FM and FM stereo received with control console, BSR automatic changer, matching wide-width and range speakers, stereo headphones, 8-track player and recorder deck. It has extra sensitive woofers and tewtters for stereo buffs who appreciate the best. It records from radio, television or anything else. Automatic or manual controls, including shut-off at the end. I'll take $500 or best offer by 5 p.m. Friday. Call Roy Ringle at 785-2153.

Chapter 15

Consumer Magazines

Introduction

One of the most interesting advertising media is consumer magazines. This is due in part to the wide variety of individual magazines and to the rapidity with which magazines come and go. Many magazines never appear again after publishing the first issue with great fanfare and much promise. Then, there are the longshots that do find a niche to fill and go on to flourish and build huge circulations.

As a print medium, magazines have many of the benefits of other print media. They can show the product, use long copy, and include such options as coupons, inserts, and product samples.

In addition, though, magazines have their own special features. They are printed on quality paper, which makes possible excellent reproduction. This means they can provide high-quality color reproduction. When interesting editorial content is added, many magazines gain a high degree of respect and prestige with both readers and advertisers. Magazines usually have a longer life than other advertising media. Many are collected and saved for years.

Most magazine advertisements look somewhat different from those in other print media. They often feature a single product in a large, single illustration (picture-window layout). Usually, the illustration is a photograph. More often than not, color is used. Copy can range from none to long, but usually it is modest in length. Magazine ads can more readily use emotional appeals, in contrast to ads in newspapers and business publications, which tend to be more factual and straightforward.

While newspapers and broadcast media accumulate their total audience in a day, or instantaneously, magazines build up and maintain their sales impact over a period of time, reflecting the special value of long life. Research studies indicate that a typical weekly magazine continues to build its measured audience of prime prospects over an eight-week period. A monthly magazine continues to generate additional measured readers for 12 weeks after publication.

According to the Magazine Publishers Association, 94 percent of U.S. adults read magazines during the average month, and these readers are motivated to act as a result of reading. Twenty percent write or phone in for more information on advertised products, and 62 percent discuss the articles they've read with someone else. They read and reread the copy in magazine ads and usually keep issues on hand for future reference.

Advantages

The tangible advantages of magazine advertising don't change from year to year. They pertain primarily to the image of magazines as a mass medium, the typical responses of readers, and certain characteristics of the ads themselves.

Image

Magazines are widely considered a necessity rather than a luxury. This is because they satisfy the need to know—in depth. And they cater to special personal interests as no other medium does. Thus, magazines create their own environment. As a result, the advertiser purchases a frame of mind as well as a frame of reference for his ads. Magazines are also generally thought of as credible. More than 60 percent of the people surveyed rated magazine advertising believable. Less than 40 percent rated television advertising believable. In addition, magazines are convenient. They are take-alongs that fit into briefcases and tote bags for the beach, the boat, the train, and the plane.

Readers

Magazines tend to attract loyal readers. For this reason, they aren't easily ignored. According to research studies, the increase in advertising pages has had no effect on the level of advertising readership. It's as high as ever. Also, magazine ads seem to enjoy high recall. They aren't easily forgotten. In fact, Gallup Robinson found that magazine advertising recall is on the rise. Finally, magazines get reader response. They are not passive. Opinion Research Corporation discovered that the prime prospects for most products are more likely to respond to a magazine ad than to a television commercial.

Magazines help the advertiser select his audience carefully. They are the number-one medium when it comes to zeroing in on prime prospects who are in the market for a particular product. Almost one out of five magazines runs in either a regional or demographic edition.

Ads

Because magazine readers aren't limited by a stopwatch, a magazine ad can deliver its selling point in depth, in as many words as it takes. Magazines can put a coupon, a message, an offer, a recipe right in a prospect's hands—to be saved, read, mailed in, and acted on. Magazine ads have a long-term effect. Direct-response advertisers have proved that a magazine ad can produce results six months—and even a year—after publication.

General Guidelines

There is a broad spectrum of magazines, serving almost every interest imaginable, from which the consumer may choose (see Exhibit 15-1). And, unlike television, where the advertising bears little or no relationship to the programing, magazine ads tend to be compatible with, and even enhanced by, the editorial environment of the magazine. This means, obviously, that

EXHIBIT **15-1.** 50 Leading A.B.C. Magazines*

(Based on average circulation per issue, 2nd six months of 1980)

Rank		Circulation	% Change vs. 1979
1	TV Guide	17,981,657	− 5.6
2	Reader's Digest	17,898,681	+ 0.1
3	National Geographic	10,711,886	+ 2.9
4	Better Homes & Gardens	8,052,693	− 0.6
5	Woman's Day	7,748,069	+ 2.5
6	Family Circle	7,529,734	− 2.9
7	AARP News Bulletin	6,762,921	NA
8	Modern Maturity	6,748,925	NA
9	McCall's	6,218,169	− 4.7
10	Ladies Home Journal	5,601,449	+ 1.8
11	Good Housekeeping	5,290,833	+ 0.4
12	National Enquirer	5,051,496	+ 0.5
13	Playboy	5,011,099	− 4.5
14	Time	4,358,911	+ 2.0
15	Redbook	4,353,745	+ 1.2
16	Penthouse	4,330,949	− 8.1
17	The Star	3,508,558	+ 6.6
18	Newsweek	2,964,279	+ 1.0
19	Cosmopolitan	2,837,325	+ 3.3
20	American Legion	2,599,187	+ 0.3
21	People	2,499,573	+10.4
22	Prevention	2,429,439	+10.1
23	Sports Illustrated	2,265,760	− 0.4
24	U.S. News & World Report	2,055,993	+ 0.6
25	Field & Stream	2,021,599	0.0
26	Glamour	1,935,636	+ 3.0
27	Popular Science	1,933,262	+ 7.4
28	Smithsonian	1,904,515	+ 5.1
29	V.F.W. Magazine	1,844,891	+ 0.9
30	Globe	1,802,988	+16.1
31	Southern Living	1,783,152	− 4.3
32	Outdoor Life	1,733,692	+ 1.4
33	Popular Mechanics	1,677,303	+ 2.1
34	Elks Magazine	1,651,862	+ 0.4
35	Today's Education	1,651,783	− 2.5
36	Mechanix Illustrated	1,626,182	− 3.2
37	Seventeen	1,552,884	+ 7.1
38	Parents	1,515,707	+ 4.1
39	Workbasket	1,472,139	− 6.2
40	Boy's Life	1,462,745	− 3.5
41	True Story	1,432,900	−10.7
42	Hustler	1,420,678	−16.5
43	Sunset	1,417,304	+ 1.0
44	Changing Times	1,407,690	+14.1
45	Life	1,338,026	+ 0.5
46	Organic Gardening	1,335,699	NA
47	Ebony	1,287,670	+ 2.0
48	Nation's Business	1,265,555	+ 0.7
49	New Woman	1,251,595	+ 4.7
50	Sport	1,222,718	+ 1.3

*Includes general and farm magazines of the Audit Bureau of Circulation.

SOURCE: Magazine Publisher Association.

the copywriter creating an ad must bear in mind the specific magazine in which the ad will appear. The audience varies from one magazine to another; so he or she will write in different styles for ads in different magazines.

The copywriter should know that the type and amount of information in magazine advertising is usually different from that in other media. Magazines generally emphasize product information—all the quality details, the performance, etc.—that provides the ongoing sales persuasion needed to build and sustain successful campaigns. All this information can be included in an ad because a magazine can hold a reader for comparatively long periods of time—long enough to fill out a coupon, write a check, or phone in an order.

Specific Guidelines

Many ads are passed over, or only partially read, because the copy ignores simple principles of easy readability.

As an advertising copywriter, your job is to capture and hold the attention of your readers. People may be thinking about other things when they see your ad. It is up to you to be so interesting, so challenging, and so distinctive that you compel their full attention. It is only then that you earn your salary as a copywriter.

Remember, you are in trust of the money the client is spending. If your ad fails to stop and hold the reader, you are wasting the client's money.

Here are some principles to keep in mind for writing effective copy—copy that will be read and will initiate action.

- Begin with your strongest consumer benefit.
- Write to the educational and cultural level of your selected audience.
- Give your copy news value. Put news into the first paragraph.
- Speedily identify copy with the needs and desires of readers.
- Don't clutter copy with too many minor claims.
- Strive for 100 percent clarity.
- Avoid ambiguity and words of doubtful meaning.
- Substitute concrete words for abstract words.
- Try to use short sentences, not longer than 14 or 15 words.
- Try to use short paragraphs of not more than four or five lines of type.
- Use vivid present tense, singular rather than plural.
- Avoid too many adjectives, adverbs, and dependent clauses.
- Lead carefully and logically from one point of interest to the next.
- Stick to the theme. Don't wander away from it.
- Don't start too many sentences with "the" or "these" or "it."
- Be credible and avoid exaggerated claims.
- Eliminate cliches, bromides, and hackneyed expressions. Because they are dull and boring, they lose the reader.
- Don't make the copy longer than is needed to impart essential information. Be lively. Be compact. Be brisk.
- Remember that it takes hard writing to make easy reading.

EXHIBIT **15-2.** Magazine Checklist and Evaluation

	Very Good	Good	Fair	Weak	Very Weak
RATIONALE:					
1. Prospect analysis	[ ]	[ ]	[ ]	[ ]	[ ]
2. Advertisement analysis	[ ]	[ ]	[ ]	[ ]	[ ]
LAYOUT:					
1. Layout format appropriate?	[ ]	[ ]	[ ]	[ ]	[ ]
2. Layout have flow? Balance?	[ ]	[ ]	[ ]	[ ]	[ ]
3. Use of white space	[ ]	[ ]	[ ]	[ ]	[ ]
4. Illustration interesting, with impact	[ ]	[ ]	[ ]	[ ]	[ ]
5. Illustration tied to head and copy	[ ]	[ ]	[ ]	[ ]	[ ]
HEADLINE:					
1. Relates benefit	[ ]	[ ]	[ ]	[ ]	[ ]
2. Product/service name in head	[ ]	[ ]	[ ]	[ ]	[ ]
COPY:					
1. Copy interesting and readable	[ ]	[ ]	[ ]	[ ]	[ ]
2. Copy claims believable	[ ]	[ ]	[ ]	[ ]	[ ]
3. Copy complete	[ ]	[ ]	[ ]	[ ]	[ ]
4. Asks for action	[ ]	[ ]	[ ]	[ ]	[ ]
5. Relates back to headline idea	[ ]	[ ]	[ ]	[ ]	[ ]
MISCELLANEOUS:					
1. Mechanics					
A. Lettering	[ ]	[ ]	[ ]	[ ]	[ ]
B. Sketching/tracing	[ ]	[ ]	[ ]	[ ]	[ ]
C. Copy blocks lined and keyed	[ ]	[ ]	[ ]	[ ]	[ ]
2. Overall idea and ad	[ ]	[ ]	[ ]	[ ]	[ ]
3. Spelling and grammar	[ ]	[ ]	[ ]	[ ]	[ ]
4. Followed directions (on time, etc.)	[ ]	[ ]	[ ]	[ ]	[ ]

COMMENTS:

EXHIBIT **15-3.** Magazine Ads

Liquor, beer, and perfume ads are notorious for showing the product alone, with minimal copy. Revlon's Charlie relies almost solely on its name and an evocative illustration. Kodak, Amaretto di Saronno, and Michelob focus on the product and limit copy to a one-sentence headline.

SOURCES: Courtesy of *Advertising Age;* courtesy of Eastman Kodak Company; courtesy of Foreign Vintages, Inc.; Michelob Beer, Agency: D'Arcy-MacManus & Masius/St. Louis.

Long-copy ads are appropriate for products with special features or distinctive attributes. When the consumer is primarily interested in utility, the ad should emphasize substance over style, information over entertainment.

Protect Your Corporation's Tax Shelter Status Without A Lawyer

WHY OUR VERSION OF A BMW OUTPERFORMS EVERYONE ELSE'S.

IMPORTANT NEWS...

Arm & Hammer® Pure Baking Soda is proven to remove plaque.

Ask your dentist why that's important.

To remove plaque better, it takes Arm & Hammer and you.

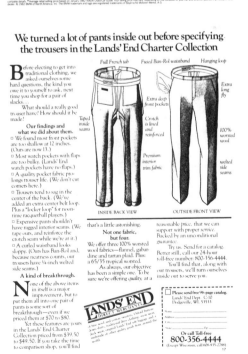

We turned a lot of pants inside out before specifying the trousers in the Lands' End Charter Collection

Or call Toll-free
800-356-4444

SOURCES: T. N. Peterson, copywriter for Enterprise Advertising, Inc.; courtesy of BMW of North America; courtesy of *Advertising Age*; courtesy of Land's End.

ASSIGNMENT **15-1.**   Writing a Magazine Ad

Name the new product described below, determine which magazines to use, and create a full-page, introductory ad for the magazines you have chosen.

For this particular exercise, let us invent a new product. It is an electric razor for men, which needs no battery and does not have to be plugged in. It can be used anywhere, anytime.

The _____ shaves razor-close; but it will not nick, cut, or scrape because of its exclusive feature, the "Face-Guard." It is extremely gentle on the skin, guaranteed not to cause any irritation. Other advantages are: quietness, works at high speed with minimal noise and little or no vibration. It is light, compact, easy to hold, and fits easily in the palm of the hand. Cleaning is quick and simple.

The _____ comes with a separate shaving head for sideburns and safe, easy moustache trimming.

The _____ has a lifetime guarantee.

ASSIGNMENT **15-2.**   Writing a Magazine Ad

Tourism in the United States is big business, and so is the advertising to promote it. An estimated $20,000,000 is spent annually on travel advertising, with magazines as the leading ad medium. Many cities have special tourist departments set up for the specific purpose of promoting the influx of travelers from other areas; tourists who stay awhile at a motel or hotel and take advantage of local attractions. An effective campaign can significantly increase tourism. For instance, the "I Love New York" promotion is credited with a 19 percent increase in tourism income for that city.

Travel ads, often prepared by ad agencies, appear regularly in consumer magazines. Obviously, these ads present the specific attractions the particular locale has to offer. If the advertising campaign does its job effectively, the result is increased revenue for hotel and motel owners, night clubs, restaurants, bars, amusement parks, theaters, sports, recreational facilities, and business in general.

It should be borne in mind that the trouble with many tourist ads is their sameness, their "look-alike" quality. And there's no excuse for such lame and pallid advertising. The copywriter, if he does his research properly, should find no difficulty in finding the U.S.P. (Unique Selling Proposition) for such an ad. Then, he should use that U.S.P. to show readers the distinctive differences and advantages that make his city the best possible choice.

Do copy and layout for a full-page consumer magazine ad. Select a specific city, such as New York, Denver, San Francisco, Boston, Chicago, New Orleans, Sante Fe, Seattle, Phoenix, or choose any city with which you are familiar and which lends itself to a tourist ad. An alternative is to create such an ad for a foreign city or country.

Chapter 16

Business Publications

Introduction

Business publications are periodicals with editorial content aimed at a specific business, industry, trade, occupation, or professional group. Most of them are presented in magazine format, but many appear in newspaper format.

Many business publications have controlled circulations. This means they have a policy of restricting distribution to people in a clearly defined group. The reason for this policy is to reduce costs by holding down the circulation of the publication. Only people who have a professional interest in the publication receive it.

There are two basic kinds of business publications—vertical and horizontal. Vertical publications are those that deal with a specific industry and its closely allied fields, at all levels of activity and management. For example, *Camping Industry, Advertising Age,* and *Milling & Baking News* are vertical business publications. Horizontal publications are those focusing on a specific job function that cuts across industry lines. Examples are *Computer Design, Purchasing,* and *Institutional Management.*

Types of Business Publications

Business publications may be classified in many ways. *Business Publication Rates and Data* lists over 150 categories, ranging from "Advertising and Marketing" and "Air Conditioning" to "Wire & Wire Products" and "Woodworking." But these can be collapsed into six major groups:

1. **Industrial.** Deal primarily with production and manufacturing.
   a. *Iron Age*
   b. *Oil & Gas Journal*
   c. *Rubber & Plastics News*

2. **Trade.** Go to dealers, distributors, jobbers and other middlemen.
   a. *Men's Wear*
   b. *American Druggist*
   c. *The Wholesaler*

3. **Professional.** Edited for people in the professions.
   a. Medicine: *Modern Medicine*
   b. Law: *The Practical Lawyer*

     c. Education: *Today's Education*
     d. Architecture: *Architectural Record*

4. **Institutions.** Edited for people who work for institutions.
     a. Hospitals: *Hospital Progress*
     b. Hotels: *Hotel & Motel Management*
     c. Organizations: *AIA Journal*

5. **General business:** Edited for all business people.
     a. *Business Week*
     b. *Fortune*
     c. *Barron's*

6. **Agriculture.** Edited for the farmers and ranchers as producers as well as consumers. Most agricultural publications are listed in the *Consumer Magazines SRDS,* but those dealing with suppliers of agriculture products are listed in the *Business Publications SRDS.*
     a. *The Dairyman*
     b. *Agri Finance*
     c. *Farm Industry News*
     d. *Farm Store Merchandising*
     e. *Feed & Grain Times*
     f. *Fertilizer Progress*

Guidelines

Advertisements in business publications retain many of the characteristics of other print media, including consumer magazines. However, they tend to follow a few basic approaches that appear to have worked well in this medium. Some of the more common ones are:

- Case histories (third person)
- Testimonials (first person)
- Problem-solution formats
- Demonstrations (e.g., torture tests)
- Before-after comparisons

In addition, business publication ads typically include elements and devices not always used in other media, such as:

- Long copy
- Technical specialized language
- Diagrams, charts, graphs
- Cutaway and ghost drawings
- Two-color (spot color) instead of full color
- Action devices (coupon, address, telephone number)

Although emotional appeals are used less often in business ads than in consumer ads, the business publication reader doesn't simply turn off his or her emotions while reading. Still, copy and appeals tend to be more serious and straightforward, often using more facts and figures than consumer ads use. Readers tend to prefer the rational to the emotional approach in headlines and body copy. Additionally, the copy should be more specific than general.

Unlike consumer copy, which may be very brief and often features a dominant illustration and almost no copy at all (perfume ads, liquor ads, etc.), the copy in business advertising may be quite lengthy and detailed. However, the copywriter should not permit himself to lapse into self-indulgent whimsy or cuteness. He must keep in mind that his reader wants facts and wants them presented lucidly.

The need to present benefits is one of the oldest and soundest principles of advertising. And nowhere is it more important than in business publication ads. There is no room for fuzziness. When copy gets too clever or the layout is cluttered or gimmicked up, the reader has trouble getting the message because he refuses to do the extra mental work required. So, the copy should be newsworthy and informative. It should relate to problems the reader needs to solve.

Although the copy should be straightforward, it should not be dull. It can present the facts in detail but still be creative and dramatic and convey its story with telling impact.

EXHIBIT **16-1.** Business Publication Checklist and Evaluation

	Very Good	Good	Fair	Weak	Very Weak
RATIONALE:					
1. Prospect analysis	[ ]	[ ]	[ ]	[ ]	[ ]
2. Advertisement analysis	[ ]	[ ]	[ ]	[ ]	[ ]
LAYOUT:					
1. Layout format appropriate?	[ ]	[ ]	[ ]	[ ]	[ ]
2. Layout have flow? Balance?	[ ]	[ ]	[ ]	[ ]	[ ]
3. Use of white space	[ ]	[ ]	[ ]	[ ]	[ ]
4. Illustration interesting, with impact	[ ]	[ ]	[ ]	[ ]	[ ]
5. Illustration tied to head and copy	[ ]	[ ]	[ ]	[ ]	[ ]
HEADLINE:					
1. Relates benefit	[ ]	[ ]	[ ]	[ ]	[ ]
2. Product/service name in head	[ ]	[ ]	[ ]	[ ]	[ ]
COPY:					
1. Testimonial, case history, how to	[ ]	[ ]	[ ]	[ ]	[ ]
2. Copy claims believable	[ ]	[ ]	[ ]	[ ]	[ ]
3. Copy complete	[ ]	[ ]	[ ]	[ ]	[ ]
4. Asks for action	[ ]	[ ]	[ ]	[ ]	[ ]
5. Relates back to headline idea	[ ]	[ ]	[ ]	[ ]	[ ]
MISCELLANEOUS:					
1. Mechanics					
A. Lettering	[ ]	[ ]	[ ]	[ ]	[ ]
B. Sketching/tracing	[ ]	[ ]	[ ]	[ ]	[ ]
C. Copy blocks lined and keyed	[ ]	[ ]	[ ]	[ ]	[ ]
2. Overall idea and ad	[ ]	[ ]	[ ]	[ ]	[ ]
3. Spelling and grammar	[ ]	[ ]	[ ]	[ ]	[ ]
4. Followed directions (on time, etc.)	[ ]	[ ]	[ ]	[ ]	[ ]

COMMENTS:

EXHIBIT 16-2. Business Publication Ads

Although neither shows the product, these two-page spreads reveal two different approaches to business-to-business advertising. Hewlett-Packard relies on a straightforward "customer reference" stressing product applications. Lanier uses a metaphor with multiple meanings in both copy and illustration.

What if you chose Hewlett-Packard as a <u>business</u> computer partner?

"At Kirke-Van Orsdel, an HP computer network speeds data processing fivefold."

Kirke-Van Orsdel in Des Moines, Iowa, is the nation's largest insurance broker/administrator for national associations.

Senior Vice President Donald Brandt says, "Our network of HP 3000 computers has enabled us to increase our business volume 50-fold in just five years. How? First, we can handle data five times faster than with our previous system, so premiums and applications are processed the same day they're received. Second, computerized claims processing enables our adjuster to handle over 100 claims per day; twice the claims most competitors can. And third, we can expand the network without costly programming.

"With the HP network, we have gained a competitive edge in both service and price."

"At Global International, an HP computer network cuts data processing costs in half."

Global International moves households across the nation and around the world. From company headquarters in Anaheim, California, two HP 3000 computers manage communications, with 100 HP terminals distributing real-time information to Global offices throughout the U.S.

Andrew Butterbrodt, company treasurer, says, "With our HP computer network we know the location and status of any shipment, any time. And because we're managing information more effectively, we've eliminated redundant processing and costly outside DP services—cutting our costs by as much as 50 percent.

"With the HP system we're able to meet a greater scope of customer needs and service our accounts with confidence. The result? A 16 percent increase in sales."

What should you expect from a computer partner?

Quality—from researching customer needs to product development, manufacturing, marketing, after-sales service, and support!

Quality, by HP's definition, encompasses more than the product.

This high quality recently was recognized by the Union of Japanese Scientists & Engineers, who awarded a coveted Deming Prize to Yokogawa-Hewlett-Packard, HP's joint venture company in Japan.

YHP offers the entire spectrum of HP products and in 1981 accounted for Japanese sales of more than $200 million. Nearly 60 percent of the products YHP sells are imported from HP manufacturing operations

The Deming Prize: for outstanding merit in the control of quality.

in the US and abroad. Conversely, YHP manufactures and exports various products to HP customers throughout the world.

The total quality control approach for which YHP was awarded the Deming Prize is a point of pride throughout HP. Customers in every part of the world should expect quality as a fundamental element in a computer partnership with HP.

You should consider a working partnership with HP. Now.

For a free copy of our brochure explaining HP's practical, proven approach to meeting your long-term computer and information needs, write to A. P. Oliverio, Senior Vice President, Marketing, Dept. 207, Hewlett-Packard Company, P.O. Box 10301, Palo Alto, CA 94303.

When performance must be measured by results **[hp] HEWLETT PACKARD**

To be a success, you can't hide in the woods.

MOVE AHEAD AT THE SPEED OF SOUND **LANIER THOUGHT PROCESSING**

SOURCES: Courtesy of Hewlett-Packard Company; Courtesy of Lanier Business Products, Inc., Thought Processing Division.

EXHIBIT **16-2.** Business Publication Ads (continued)

Like Lanier, Burroughs summarizes a "problem" and urges readers to write to the company for a solution. With a drawn illustration and maximum white space, Foote, Cone & Belding conveys simplicity and informality in both words and picture. Sony shows its product (life-size) and describes product features.

"If I can get it through my ACD before the CD sees it, we might be able to catch the ECD and schedule an ARB. So how're things over at FCB?"

Simpler.
We've cut out the middlemen and done away with the alphabet soup.
We don't have a lot of empty titles and a lot of supervisors and a lot of hassle.
This is pretty much a place where you show it to the boss, and then you show it to the client. At FCB, controlling the work is back where it belongs.
With the workers.

FCB
FOOTE, CONE & BELDING
401 N. Michigan Avenue/Chicago

"INFORMANIA"
It's having to decide with absolute, total uncertainty.

You face a clear-cut decision.
You either increase production or you don't.
Which is to say you either succeed or you fail. Such decisions are your life's work.
So when you've got to sign on the line, but there's not a scrap of hard evidence to help you, momentary loss of vision is entirely normal.
That's "Informania."
The solution is information. The right information. In the right form. For the right people in the right place and time.
Burroughs can help. Because we know how to manage information. We've put 95 years of thought and experience into it. We offer a comprehensive solution to the problem of "Informania."
Our computers and office automation systems can help you collect, compose, analyze, store, recall, reformulate and distribute information.
So that you will know. And act with certainty.
When "Informania" strikes, the answer is Burroughs. Write for our brochure: Burroughs Corporation, Dept. WSJ-19, Burroughs Place, Detroit, Michigan 48232.

Burroughs
Building on strength

Presenting
Betamax Components.
(actual size)

If you've been looking for the video system of your dreams, stand this magazine on your bookshelf. Or your TV set. Or next to your hi-fi equipment.
And see how it looks. Look how it fits.
This is the actual size of Sony's amazing Betamax Component System.
Combined, the Recorder and the Tuner/Timer give you all the features you could ask for in a home video unit.
There's BetaScan for high speed picture search. Swing Search for reviewing in normal and slow speeds, forward and reverse.
There's a Linear Time Tape Counter that shows recording and playback time in hours, minutes and seconds.
The Tuner/Timer gives you Sony's Express Tuning System and 2-week, 4-event unattended programming.
Then there's the wireless Remote Commander. It lets you perform all the important functions, including special effects, without moving from your chair.
Finally, with Sony's Trinicon Color Camera, you can turn your home unit into a portable one.
Besides the finest resolution, low-light sensitivity, and true color reproduction, this camera gives you

a host of little miracles.
There's an electronic viewfinder that shows you exactly what you're shooting and lets you review your last shot and plan your next with perfect transition at the touch of a button.
There's also remote control capability, a built-in microphone, a motor-driven macro-zoom lens, automatic settings and an almost endless variety of accessories.
As a special introductory offer, if you buy the SL-2000 Recorder before August 31, 1982, we'll give you six free Sony video cassettes and a guide to portable video recording. They're worth over $100 and give you up to 18 hours of recording.
When you buy the Betamax Recorder and Trinicon Camera together, we'll give you 12 cassettes worth over $200.
So hurry down to your participating Sony dealer and look for the display that looks like this ad. There, you'll be able to play with the complete range of components and accessories.
And you'll be able to do what the whole Betamax Component System was designed for in the first place. You'll be able to pick one up.

SONY.
THE ONE AND ONLY

ASSIGNMENT **16-1.**   Writing a Business Publication Ad

Create a full-page ad (copy and layout) for a midwestern, monthly farm publication.

> The product is a vitamin D derivative for prevention of milk fever in dairy cows. A campaign in farm journals is about to be launched to show how this product can combat the disease.
>
> Milk fever is caused by a calcium deficiency and often occurs after the second calving. Cows become weak, lose control of muscles, develop low body temperature, and may become unconscious. With proper treatment, a cow may recover from milk fever, but productive capacity remains lower and productive life is shorter than normal.
>
> The product, PMF-125, prevents milk fever if injected intramuscularly 72 hours before calving. One injection protects for a week. Since about 8 percent of all dairy cows get milk fever, the market is large enough to warrant the introduction of a new product, which faces no direct competition.
>
> Two of the early objectives are (1) to determine whether marketing through veterinarians is profitable and (2) to ascertain the use according to herd sizes and production levels.
>
> The advertising goals are to impress upon dairy farmers that:
>
> 1. There is a preventative for milk fever: PMF-125
> 2. PMF-125 is economical and easy to use
> 3. PMF-125 is low-cost insurance against normal treatment costs for milk fever and the risk of losing the cow
> 4. Use of PMF-125 reduces worry and work

Chapter 17

Direct Mail

Introduction

Direct mail is the use of mailed advertising to deliver an advertiser's message directly to selected individuals and business organizations. Properly coordinated with other advertising media, it can increase their effectiveness. For an advertiser whose promotional funds may be limited, it can be, and frequently is, the primary or sole advertising medium. Manufacturers, wholesalers, retailers, publishers, mail-order houses, insurance companies, fund raisers, public utilities, and financial services all use direct mail as an integral part of their business.

Despite the layman's snide reference to "junk mail," direct mail is the third largest advertising medium in the United States, topped only by newspaper and television advertising. Billions of dollars are spent on its various forms annually, and the investment in direct mail grows each year. It includes a variety of formats: letters, booklets, brochures, folders, circulars, postcards, catalogs, coupons, novelties and many other forms of materials designed to reach specific firms and people. Unlike other media that may have to scatter their shots, direct mail can, when properly used, reach its prospects with pinpoint efficiency.

Direct Mail vs. Direct Response

There is a difference between direct mail and direct response—and a very distinct one. Direct mail, very simply, uses the mail. Direct response uses many other media: newspapers, magazines, statement stuffers, on-pack promotions, radio, television—just about every medium except skywriting.

Direct response is a way of selling that uses one or more communications media for the purpose of getting a response to the sender (or advertiser) directly from the reader, viewer, or listener.

The primary objectives of direct mail are to produce a sale, produce an inquiry, and generate store traffic. Direct mail often uses a letter, in addition to other enclosures. In some instances, it may use a letter alone. This is often true in solicitations for charitable causes. (For an example, see Exhibit 17-1.)

Advantages

Direct mail is effective because it can be controlled and regulated, it allows for maximum flexibility, and it has wide appeal.

EXHIBIT **17-1.** A Direct Mail Solicitation*

American Foundation for the Blind, Inc.

Good Neighbor:

Just shut your eyes and run your fingers along the raised dots on the enclosed calendar. This will show you how blind people can look up a date in advance.

But using a braille pocket calendar is not quite as simple as this may sound. Let me explain.

Braille is bulky. Consequently, this little calendar is only a reference tool. It has on it the word *Calendar*, the year, and the day of the week on which the first day of each month falls. That's all—no more. If it had every day of every month on it like the usual pocket calendar underneath it, it would be 12 pages long and 4 by 5½ inches in size.

Naturally, a blind person cannot tuck a bulky article like that in his pocket, so he must calculate the rest of the dates mentally. For example, he must remember that the eighth, fifteenth, twenty-second and twenty-ninth of a month always fall on the same day of the week as the first day of that month.

But enough of that. Blind people often are required to make greater use of their memories and sense of touch than you do. In addition, they count heavily on their sense of hearing.

These then are some of the clues on how thousands of blind Americans compensate to make up for lack of sight. And they look to this national research and resource center to find newer and better ways to help them to do this. Please do give today and keep the doorway to progress for blind people at AFB wide open. We will be grateful to you all year long.

Very sincerely yours,

*The mailing included a pocket-sized braille calendar.

Control

Mailing lists afford greater selectivity than any other advertising medium. The advertiser can target his message to almost any demographic category, including age group, profession, and even area of residence. Time of mailing can be precisely regulated. And response can be accurately measured, simply by counting reply cards, envelopes, or order blanks.

With the proper mailing list (which is usually readily available), there is little waste circulation. Nevertheless, it must be kept in mind that direct mail may arrive unsolicited and even unwanted. It is, obviously, of vital importance that the writer and artist combine their creative talents to produce a piece that captures the eye, the mind, and the interest of the recipient. And this is where creative ingenuity plays its part.

Flexibility

Direct mail gives the advertiser greater flexibility than any other print medium in choice of format, selection of material, and reproduction process. Virtually anything that can be printed—from an order form on a postcard to an elaborate combination of words and pictures in a brochure—can be used. In addition, direct mail can be employed as a research tool, as well as an advertising medium. Different appeals, ideas, and copy variations can be tested prior to a major expenditure.

In direct mail, the copywriter need not be concerned about writing copy that is too long. He usually has all the space he needs to give his reader all the benefits he can truthfully and convincingly convey. But, of course, long copy can become dull. If, however, the copy is lively and scintillating, it is amazing how much the reader will actually wade through. Research has proved that long copy, if well done and with strong presentation of specific consumer benefits, will be read—and will initiate action.

Appeal

Direct mail is the most personal of all advertising media. If the recipient's name appears on the envelope, a bond is immediately established. Furthermore, although many people denigrate direct mail (as "junk mail"), most people open and read whatever kind of mail they receive. There is no competition for the reader's attention, as there is in radio or television or newspapers (except for the mail that arrives with the direct mail piece).

General Guidelines

How does the copywriter induce people to pay attention to a piece of direct mail they've just received? It may be from a company they've never heard of, and it may be selling a product they never thought of buying.

Perhaps the first thing the copywriter must do to capture attention and sustain interest is to give the prospect news. News interests people, and despite the fact that many products aren't intrinsically newsworthy, he must create or at least imbue the ordinary item with a special aura. Take heed of the ancient advertising adage, "Sell the sizzle, not the steak."

But that's only the beginning. For now, the copywriter must obtain conviction, which depends almost entirely on believability. Therefore, it is important not to oversell or exaggerate. While these warnings apply to all advertising in all media, they are particularly applicable to direct mail. An ad in a magazine or newspaper attains some credibility merely because it appears in the publication in close proximity to editorial matter, which is allegedly factual. This advantage does not apply to the unsolicited letter or brochure that arrives in the mail.

However, direct mail does have the great advantage of being able to ask for and to initiate action. This "asking" should be done in bold strokes. Tell the reader just what you want him to do. If it's an actual order you can get through the mail, don't be subtle about it—ask for it. If you don't ask in clear, precise terms, you may not pierce the prospect's apathy. And make action easy. Enclose a postage-paid, preaddressed envelope. Include a toll-free telephone number for instant ordering or to gain additional information. At least, add a coupon, which asks for all the necessary information. You can further induce action by limiting the time of the offer or stating that quantities are limited.

Direct mail is a highly personal form of communication. It's almost like writing a letter. (After all, it does arrive in the mail.) In fact, a letter is commonly enclosed as part of the direct mail "package." The letter should not be loosely written, with long, wandering sentences and paragraphs. Copy should have a natural, conversational tone. Of course, effective copy abides by the rules of grammar and uses correct syntax. However, you can, if you're careful, adhere to the principles of good writing without sounding pretentious or stuffy.

In order to maintain the personal touch, use the second person throughout. Be personal, but not overbearing. Write as though you're addressing an acquaintance. But be wary about getting too cozy or too cute, because then you run the danger of "writing down." If you write down, you may have a resentful reader, and resentment leads to resistance.

Specific Guidelines

Here are some more specific guidelines for preparing a direct mail piece:

Describe selling points completely. You have the space to say everything you can think of about your product or service. Take advantage of it by repeating the product points in different and various ways. One point may appeal to one person while another may not. Be specific. Give explicit instructions and descriptions.

Emphasize major benefits. Be sure to tell the reader how the product or service will benefit him. These prospect points are the primary and secondary wants and needs of all humans. So relating them to your product or service will possibly induce action.

Offer something free or at a low price. By offering something free (specified or "surprise") you increase the number of responses. It may be something extra (a gift) or extended (an additional month's subscription). It could be a self-liquidating premium for which a low price is charged.

Include a guarantee. If possible, offer a guarantee, warranty, or money-back proposition. People are increasingly more wary—particularly of buying sight unseen—and want some assurance of protection.

Don't overlook the envelope. Perhaps the most critical moment in a direct mail piece's life is when it first arrives. Does it get opened or thrown away? The envelope will have a great deal to do with that decision. Design this piece carefully. Consider the paper, color, typeface, addressing method (hand, machine, etc.), and postage procedure (stamp, meter). And don't overlook the possibility of adding a message of enticement to the envelope. It may help in stopping the reader and getting him to look inside.

EXHIBIT **17-2.** Direct Mail Checklist and Evaluation

	Very Good	Good	Fair	Weak	Very Weak
RATIONALE:					
1. Prospect analysis	[ ]	[ ]	[ ]	[ ]	[ ]
2. Advertisement analysis	[ ]	[ ]	[ ]	[ ]	[ ]
LAYOUT:					
1. Covering letter, letterhead	[ ]	[ ]	[ ]	[ ]	[ ]
2. Main piece (brochure, leaflet)	[ ]	[ ]	[ ]	[ ]	[ ]
3. Response piece	[ ]	[ ]	[ ]	[ ]	[ ]
4. Main envelope	[ ]	[ ]	[ ]	[ ]	[ ]
5. Use of color	[ ]	[ ]	[ ]	[ ]	[ ]
6. Illustrations appropriate	[ ]	[ ]	[ ]	[ ]	[ ]
HEADLINES:					
1. Relate benefits	[ ]	[ ]	[ ]	[ ]	[ ]
2. Product/service name in headlines	[ ]	[ ]	[ ]	[ ]	[ ]
COPY:					
1. Covering letter copy	[ ]	[ ]	[ ]	[ ]	[ ]
2. Main piece copy	[ ]	[ ]	[ ]	[ ]	[ ]
3. Other copy	[ ]	[ ]	[ ]	[ ]	[ ]
4. Claims believable	[ ]	[ ]	[ ]	[ ]	[ ]
5. Holds interest	[ ]	[ ]	[ ]	[ ]	[ ]
6. Asks for the order	[ ]	[ ]	[ ]	[ ]	[ ]
MISCELLANEOUS:					
1. Mechanics					
A. Lettering	[ ]	[ ]	[ ]	[ ]	[ ]
B. Sketching/tracing	[ ]	[ ]	[ ]	[ ]	[ ]
C. Copy blocks lined and keyed	[ ]	[ ]	[ ]	[ ]	[ ]
2. Overall idea and ad package	[ ]	[ ]	[ ]	[ ]	[ ]
3. Spelling and grammar	[ ]	[ ]	[ ]	[ ]	[ ]
4. Followed directions (on time, etc.)	[ ]	[ ]	[ ]	[ ]	[ ]

COMMENTS:

EXHIBIT **17-3.** Direct Mail Ads

John Blair Menswear enclosed its letter, reply card, product descriptions, and other materials in a sealed plastic envelope. The direct mail package also contained six fabric swatches, giving the recipient the real "feel" of the product.

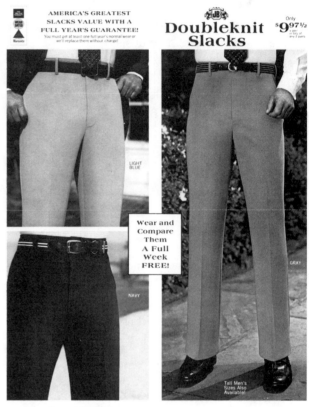

SOURCE: Courtesy of New Process Co.

The 32-page Baldwin Cooke Holiday Gift Catalog included product descriptions and illustrations, an order form, and a reply envelope. A guarantee, telephone number, and two requests for additional consumer information were included on the obverse side of the envelope.

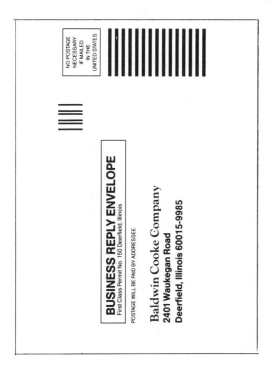

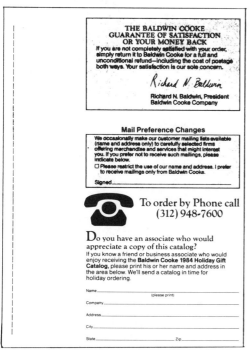

ASSIGNMENT 17-1. Planning a Direct Mail Piece

Create a theme or slogan for the following promotion. Then, on a separate sheet, list the key points to make in writing the copy for the mailing piece.

> Great Plains Telephone Company operates in 105 communities throughout Kansas, Nebraska, and western Iowa. Although it is a public utility and is normally regarded as a regulated monopoly, the company is actually confronted by competition for some of the services and systems it markets. Among these are speakerphone and touch-a-matic systems.
>
> Because of its scattered market area, GPT confines its mass media advertising to newspapers and spot TV and invests relatively heavily in targeted media, such as state business periodicals, direct mail, and specialty advertising. GPT advertising stresses the company's communications capabilities rather than the hardware being offered.
>
> Commercial markets have been analyzed and segmented by industry or profession, and one of the company's market stimulators has been assigned the task of developing a direct mail campaign to reach 500 small-practice physicians in the three-state area. The objectives of the mailing are (1) to position GPT as consultants available to aid the medical marketplace, (2) to enhance the GPT image in the face of competition, and (3) to generate sales of systems.
>
> Research has indicated that doctors constitute a difficult-to-reach audience. While they may find time to read medical journals, they tend not to be so attentive to direct mail solicitation.
>
> Research also has indicated that doctors are influenced greatly by peers in making purchasing decisions, that they have an affinity for assembling gadgetry or otherwise working with their hands, and that they tend to be inquisitive.

ASSIGNMENT 17-2. Creating a Direct Mail Package

You are a copywriter for a direct marketing agency that has as one of its accounts a large publishing company. Using the information provided below, create a mailing package to sell city directories to business owners, via a special "prepublication offer."

The markets your mailing will be used in are all cities of 100,000–200,000 population. The publisher wants the package to include an outside envelope with teaser copy; a cover letter from C. A. Smith, vice president; a Business Reply Mail order card; and a highlight sheet or pamphlet illustrating the directory features.

While the package will be used in several cities—and tailored to each market—you are to do the presentation copy for the 1985 City of Springfield (Ill.) Cross Reference Directory.

The directory will have two major sections with the following features.

Street section	Telephone section
listings arranged by street address and house number	listings arranged by telephone numbers in numerical sequence
zip code	telephone exchange
street name	personal name
personal name	telephone number
indication of new listing or new arrival	indication of new listing or new arrival
telephone number	business listing
no phone or nonpublished phone	address
house number	community designation
business listing	
total residential listings	
total business listings	
year first listed	

The prepublication price (including shipping) is $73.50 for the first copy. Additional copies ordered at the same time receive a 10 percent discount.

Orders will be billed with delivery, which will occur between November 1 and November 15. Regular price of the directory after publication will be $85.00, with no quantity discounts available.

Cross Reference Directories help business owners:

1. Find the address if they have only the phone number
2. Find the phone number if they have only the address
3. Identify new residents
4. Route deliveries more efficiently
5. Improve collections
6. Plan and execute direct mail advertising
7. Increase sales
8. Verify checks
9. Trace skips
10. Develop "neighbor" referrals

The publisher, in business for more than 30 years, prints directories for 130 United States and Canadian cities. Compiling procedure and expertise insure accurate and up-to-date information. Directories do not contain any advertising.

Company name and address: A to Z Publishers, Inc., 1234 Industrial Drive, Lincoln, Nebraska 68501 First Class Postal Permit Number 111.

Chapter 18

Outdoor

Introduction

With its beginnings tracing back to 3000 B.C., outdoor advertising is the oldest form of sales communication known to man. Since then, it has been refined and developed into what is known today as *standardized* outdoor advertising—a highly disciplined, tightly regulated medium. Standardized outdoor includes, not the millions of random-sized, multishaped "on-premise" signs that dominate business centers and shopping malls, but the 270,000 sign structures of uniform shape and dimension that are seen on streets and highways, often at some distance from commercial areas.

No other advertising medium enables the advertiser to reach so many prospects so quickly and so often. In addition, no other advertising medium even comes close in terms of cost efficiency.

Advantages

In considering the use of any form of advertising, the advertiser must analyze its selling values both in relation to its cost and in relation to the advertiser's specific marketing objectives. Besides offering the lowest cost-per-message of any major advertising medium, outdoor also offers definite advantages in flexibility, coverage, and impact.

Flexibility

Outdoor advertising is a very flexible medium in terms of cost and content. The advertiser can match his purchase with his budget by buying a single board or a "package" of boards. And they will be used exactly where and when the advertiser wants them.

Because of their size, outdoor signs can accommodate almost any kind of message: selling a full line of related products, introducing new products or packaging, tying-in national and local campaigns, and enhancing company image or identity.

Outdoor also allows the advertiser to communicate his message to his most-likely-to-buy prospects by concentrating his signs on routes most frequently used by his target audience.

Coverage

Alone among media, outdoor advertising can cover a market overnight. In a single day, it can deliver a total number of exposure opportunities equal to, or greater than, the entire population of the target market. According to a national study, a #100 sign is seen by nine out of every ten adults in an average market over a 30-day period. During this time, the advertising message reaches its prospects 31 times each.

Impact

Unlike yesterday's newspaper or last night's radio or television commercial, outdoor is there all day, every day, for as long as you want it, selling and reminding your prospects about your products.

Furthermore, the size and placement of outdoor signs offers an eye-catching impact provided by no other medium. (Where else can you find a 10-foot high container of milk or a 20-foot-long hot dog?) Unrivaled drama, bold colors, and, in the last few years, three-dimensionality make outdoor advertising particularly effective in fulfilling a wide variety of marketing goals.

Guidelines

Outdoor advertising can be a tremendously effective medium—when it is used correctly. It should be thought of as reminder advertising in which the message, of necessity, must be terse, brief, succinct.

Outdoor advertising is unique in that it must communicate a message to an audience that is in motion and at a distance that varies continuously. Therefore, those who are responsible for creating effective outdoor advertising must be cognizant of certain principles that are different from those that apply to other media.

Within these constraints, however, creative people can achieve spectacular results. They can come up with attention-arresting, eye-opening blockbusters. It is important to remember, though, that copy, illustrations, and color combinations should be created specifically for outdoor, not merely adapted from other media. Below are the principal fundamentals, which if followed, can help to increase legibility, comprehension, and impact.

Layout

Letters take their identity from certain basic shapes and variations or combinations of these shapes. The recognition of an individual letter occurs in proportion to the recognition of these shapes.

Capital letters have the greatest individual recognition value, but they tend to be read individually. Therefore, capitals usually work best for display headings that are only three or four words in length.

Lowercase letters are usually read as complete words or phrases because the eye has become accustomed to them through normal reading habits. It follows, then, that lowercase letters are more appropriate for longer headlines or sentences.

For maximum clarity in outdoor messages, colors should be bright and contrasting. Avoid pastels. Also, avoid the simultaneous use of colors with similar values, such as orange on red or blue on purple. Even some common seasonal color combinations, such as green on red or orange on black, are not good contrast pairs.

Illustrations should be big and bold, taking maximum advantage of the huge size of outdoor posters. Show even large products, such as automobiles, life-size or larger. Simplicity is recommended. This translates into few elements and uncluttered backgrounds.

As with all advertising, the product or service should be prominently displayed and identified. Product identification is vital. Make the product stand out. If the illustration is good enough, it will almost always convey the message by itself, and it may make copy unnecessary altogether.

Copy

Effective copy in outdoor must combine simplicity with brevity. Don't get too tricky. Never be verbose. Make your point quickly.

While there is no specified limit to the number of words, the copy should be concise enough to register quickly. Don't forget that outdoor messages will be viewed at distances of up to 400 feet by persons in motion.

Logic necessitates brevity, simplicity, and clarity. The viewer can absorb only a few words, so those few words must communicate your basic idea—quickly.

Effective outdoor advertising should follow these guidelines:

- Short copy—few words
- Short words
- Legible type
- Large illustrations
- Bold colors
- Simple background
- Product identification

EXHIBIT **18-1.** Outdoor Posters vs. Bulletins

Outdoor *posters* (paper pasted up) have the proportions 2¼:1 and should be drawn that way. The outdoor layout form in this manual is for posters. *Painted bulletins* are much longer, with the proportion 3½:1. Be sure to make this distinction.

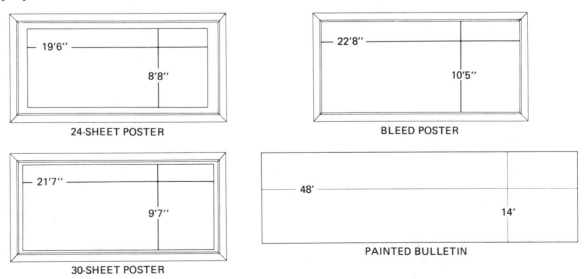

24-SHEET POSTER — 19'6" — 8'8"

BLEED POSTER — 22'8" — 10'5"

30-SHEET POSTER — 21'7" — 9'7"

PAINTED BULLETIN — 48' — 14'

EXHIBIT **18-2.** Outdoor Poster Checklist and Evaluation

	Very Good	Good	Fair	Weak	Very Weak
RATIONALE:					
1. Prospect analysis	[ ]	[ ]	[ ]	[ ]	[ ]
2. Advertisement analysis	[ ]	[ ]	[ ]	[ ]	[ ]
LAYOUT:					
1. Background simple, uncluttered?	[ ]	[ ]	[ ]	[ ]	[ ]
2. Colors bold and pertinent?	[ ]	[ ]	[ ]	[ ]	[ ]
3. Product shown?	[ ]	[ ]	[ ]	[ ]	[ ]
ILLUSTRATION:					
1. Illustration pertinent?	[ ]	[ ]	[ ]	[ ]	[ ]
2. Powerful? Have impact?	[ ]	[ ]	[ ]	[ ]	[ ]
3. Illustration large?	[ ]	[ ]	[ ]	[ ]	[ ]
COPY:					
1. Product clearly identified?	[ ]	[ ]	[ ]	[ ]	[ ]
2. Copy short?	[ ]	[ ]	[ ]	[ ]	[ ]
3. Short words? Common words?	[ ]	[ ]	[ ]	[ ]	[ ]
4. Copy have impact?	[ ]	[ ]	[ ]	[ ]	[ ]
5. Idea clear at a glance?	[ ]	[ ]	[ ]	[ ]	[ ]
6. Legible typeface?	[ ]	[ ]	[ ]	[ ]	[ ]
MISCELLANEOUS:					
1. Mechanics					
A. Lettering	[ ]	[ ]	[ ]	[ ]	[ ]
B. Sketching/tracing	[ ]	[ ]	[ ]	[ ]	[ ]
C. Color indication	[ ]	[ ]	[ ]	[ ]	[ ]
2. Overall idea and ad	[ ]	[ ]	[ ]	[ ]	[ ]
3. Spelling and grammar	[ ]	[ ]	[ ]	[ ]	[ ]
4. Followed directions	[ ]	[ ]	[ ]	[ ]	[ ]

COMMENTS:

EXHIBIT **18-3.**   Outdoor Ads

Ordinarily, outdoor ads contain only a headline and an illustration. However, as these examples show, the medium can be used for a variety of products and purposes.

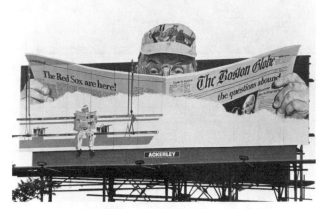

SOURCE: Courtesy of *Advertising Age.*

EXHIBIT **18-4.** Outdoor Poster Layout Forms

ASSIGNMENT 18-1.   Outdoor Poster Evaluation

Outdoor advertising is not the easiest medium to work with, but it is relatively simple in terms of having the fewest elements. There is little or no copy other than the headline. The illustration is bold and dominant. Bright colors are used. The designer strives for product identification and immediate impact.

Find an outdoor poster you consider effective and one you consider ineffective. Trace the forms provided in Exhibit 18-4 and sketch each poster as accurately as you can. Label them as effective or ineffective and write a critique of each one based on your assessment of illustration, color, and copy.

ASSIGNMENT 18-2.   Writing an Outdoor Ad

Create the copy and layout for an outdoor sign that fits the facts given below. The difficult part is to compress the information on the billboard into as few words as possible—to be succinct and yet convey pertinent information.

A new hotel has just been constructed in a medium-size midwestern city. The management has decided to advertise on an outdoor billboard located on the state highway leading into the city.

The name of the hotel is The Ambassador. It is privately owned and not part of any chain.

Location is convenient, both to the highway and to the center of the city. Rates are moderate, but not sufficiently low to warrant any special mention.

The Ambassador has an indoor-outdoor swimming pool, and each room has a color television set. There are special low rates for children under twelve.

The hotel is located on the corner of Main and 10th streets. The telephone number is 489-0092.

Bear in mind that this outdoor sign is going up in the month of May, and your advertising will appear as the tourist season begins.

Chapter 19

Transit

Introduction

Transit advertising is the kind that appears inside buses, subway cars, and commuter trains. It is also advertising that appears on subway station posters, floor exhibits, and diorama displays at train and airline terminals and on the outside of mass transit vehicles.

Transit advertising dates back to before the Civil War. It has had a colorful history and has contributed greatly to the success of such well-known brand names as Campbell's Soup, Wrigley's chewing gum, Vick's VapoRub and Ivory soap.

The first transit advertising took the form of handbills, which were suspended from the ceiling of transit vehicles by strings and hooks and then fastened to interior walls. Panel and frame display appeared in the 1860s and was in common use by the 1870s. By the 1880s, the uniformity of card advertising began to take shape in the widespread installation of display racks to hold neat rows of advertisements along the walls of vehicles. From there, it was an easy transition to the utilization of otherwise unused vehicle space.

The medium, born more than 150 years ago, has made a successful transition from the past to the present. And it appears that transit advertising will continue to occupy a key position in today's Urban Era. Its present success is due not only to its proved effectiveness but also to the energy crunch, which has forced more and more people to ride buses, trains, and subways.

Advantages

The advantages of transit advertising include:

1. An audience of prime prospects who are already out of their homes and into the buying community.
2. Excellent package identification, which can travel along with the shopper to the store.
3. Effective repetition of ads.
4. Proven readership and exposure.
5. Economy. Not only is transit advertising a low-cost medium, but it delivers repeat exposures without requiring repeat payment.
6. Other than point-of-purchase displays, transit advertising reaches buyers closer to the point of sale than any other form of advertising.

Guidelines

Copy seen on the outside of taxis, buses, and trains should, of course, be brief and succinct, almost in a headline format. Obviously, it would be foolhardy to use more than a few words in copy that appears on a moving vehicle. On the other hand, with copy that appears inside a vehicle, as on cards inside a subway car, the advertiser has what is tantamount to a captive audience. Copy here can be much longer and go into considerable detail. Research indicates that copy on subway cars gets considerable attention and is well read.

EXHIBIT **19-1.** Sizes of Transit Ads

Sizes of transit ads that appear inside buses, subway cars, and commuter trains:

11" high by 28" wide
11" high by 42" wide
11" high by 56" wide

Size of transit ads that appear on the outside of public vehicles:

21" high by 44" wide

Sizes of transit ads that appear on posters:

30" high by   83" wide
30" high by 144" wide

EXHIBIT **19-2.** Transit Ads

More than 50 years ago, buses began to carry ads inside and out. Now such ads are commonplace on all mass-transit vehicles. While many inside ads follow the minimal-copy format of outdoor ads, some use long copy for riders who have nothing to do but read them. Outside ads, however, still follow the "quick-read" format.

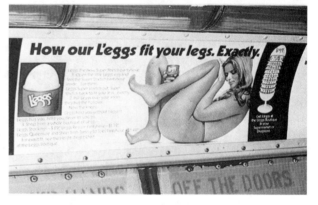

SOURCES: Courtesy of Wm. Wrigley Jr. Company; courtesy of *Advertising Age*; courtesy of Consolidated Foods Corporation, L'eggs Division. The WOOLITE® trademark and ad are the property of Boyle-Midway Division of American Home Products Corporation.

Do the layout and copy for a bus car ad that will appear in a large, metropolitan city. Consult Exhibit 19-1 for typical sizes of transit ads. Use the information given below.

> A large and successful food manufacturing company has decided to market a new product called "Sweet 'n Tart" cranberry sauce. Its marketing objective is to achieve year-round sales. Traditionally, cranberry sauce has been used by housewives on holiday occasions, such as Thanksgiving and Christmas.
>
> The advertising campaign the company is about to launch should make women think of serving cranberry sauce throughout the year, rather than merely as a sauce served with turkey. Thus, the campaign should show "Sweet 'n Tart" in association with a large variety of foods, including ham, chops, and cold cuts.
>
> In addition to women's magazines, it has been decided to use transit advertising as one of the principal media.

Chapter 20

Specialty

Introduction

Specialty advertising is much maligned and much misunderstood. It is much used and much abused. It should be considered as an advertising/sales promotion medium that utilizes articles to carry the advertiser's name, address, and advertising message to its target audience. These useful items, referred to as advertising specialties, are distributed without obligation to customers, prospects, and other groups the advertiser seeks to reach with his message.

Specialty advertising has the advantage of being able to deliver its message directly to the person who buys, the decision maker. However, the advertising specialty item itself can only transmit the message; it should not be construed as the promotion in and of itself. To be successful, it should combine originality and ingenuity. It should be useful. Above all, it should fit the theme of the entire campaign.

Although many people do not think of specialty advertising as big business, it is interesting to note that in 1981 this medium had billings of approximately $3.5 billion, which is more than was spent on any advertising medium except newspaper, television, direct mail, and radio.

Advantages

Specialty advertising is a targeted, not mass, medium. When used properly, it offers advertisers a number of advantages:

1. **Low cost per impression.**

2. **Budget flexibility.** There are literally thousands of articles of merchandise that can be used as specialties, ranging anywhere from a few cents to several hundred dollars.

3. **Targetability.** Like direct mail, specialty advertising can be directed to as narrowly defined an audience as the sponsor wishes to reach.

4. **Repetitive exposure.** Because advertising specialties are useful, they are retained.

5. **High recall.** Studies have indicated as high as 70 percent recall of sponsor's name.

These are all undoubted advantages, but there are some adverse characteristics of specialty advertising that should be mentioned. Because the specialty items are often small (wall calendars are a notable exception), there is often limited copy space. Also, specialty advertising is not a medium of intimacy. Delivery of even stock items can require several weeks, so the advertiser who wishes to deliver a message right now should probably seek another medium. Additionally, it is often difficult to measure the results of specialty advertising.

Guidelines

In order to benefit fully from the advantages of specialty advertising, copy must be carefully prepared. The first step is to determine what the item is supposed to accomplish. Copy can be used as a reminder of a convention or a business anniversary. It can be employed to herald the introduction of a new product. And while creativity is obviously restricted by space limitation, there are several guidelines to adhere to in the preparation of copy for specialty advertising.

1. **Write to the prospect's interests.** A primary consideration is the person for whom the specialty copy is intended. There is one type of copy for the homeowner, another for the seller of homes. The copy might be quite different when it is meant for a person who has just opened a savings account from when it goes to the executive vice-president of a bank.

2. **Know what you want the item to accomplish.** The copy should be related to the purpose of the specialty item. It may be copy to introduce a new product or copy in the form of an invitation to a gala party at the opening of a new business. Remember, too, the enormous flexibility you have in choosing the item itself. It can and should be geared to tie in with the business of the recipient.

3. **Copy demands will dictate item availabilities.** If you want to convey a fairly long message, your selection of specialty items will be narrowed. You will have to select an item with sufficient space for the message to be carried clearly and convincingly. For example, a ball-point pen can carry very little copy, but a calendar or even matchbooks can have considerably more.

4. **Specialty copy best serves as a reminder.** Although some advertising campaigns have used specialties as a primary or even sole advertising medium, usually they are used to supplement or complement other media. In such cases, their main function is to remind the prospect of the product or service name, address, telephone number, and slogan. When any of these are needed, they will be convenient to the prospect—in a pocket, on a desk, hanging on the wall, or pasted to the telephone.

EXHIBIT **20-1.**   Specialty Ads

Essentially "reminder" advertising, specialty is usually limited in copy—often to just the company logo. However, long copy is commonplace on such popular items as calendars and matchbook covers. Furthermore, the vehicles for carrying specialty messages are practically infinite in number.

ASSIGNMENT **20-1.** Writing a Specialty Ad

Write the copy for the calendar to be used in the campaign described below. Bear in mind that the objective is to make the reader aware of the services rendered by Homeseekers Realty and also to elicit listings.

In an industry that tends to be characterized by peaks and valleys because of seasonal demand, Homeseekers Realty finds itself in a protracted valley because of high interest rates that have turned off home buyers. As a result, residential listings for the local real estate firms have declined an average of 8 percent below the previous year, and Homeseekers must compete aggressively in a constricted market.

Harold Olson, principal of the firm, and his staff have decided to employ target media to reach the market. Selected is a target audience consisting of 500 homeowners in five different neighborhoods of the community and in five different ranges of appraised property values. Olson's objectives are to make the audience aware of Homeseekers' services and to elicit listings.

Inasmuch as there are probably only a few homeowners in the target audience who are prospective sellers at any one time, Olson is striving for repetitive exposure whereby everyone in the audience will have awareness of Homeseekers when the occasion to sell arises. For this reason, Olson has decided to employ specialty advertising. He has budgeted $1,800 for specialties and another $900 for printing of brochures and postage, because he plans to distribute the specialties and accompanying brochures by mail. He has asked his specialty advertising counselor for suggestions, including a recommendation on whether to purchase several different specialties and distribute them individually over a period of time or to use a one-shot promotion.

The specialty item to be used in this promotion is a large wall calendar that can be seen in the prospect's home all year.

Chapter 21

Yellow Pages

Introduction

The commercial telephone exchange celebrated its centennial in 1978. Less than a month after it opened in 1878, the first telephone directory appeared. It had 50 names.

All this occurred before the introduction of telephone numbers. A hundred years ago, a caller simply told the operator the name of the party he or she wanted. But even at this embryonic stage, the advantage of classified listing had become obvious—to help people avoid unnecessary searching to locate a needed product or service.

The yellow paper used to distinguish the classified directory from the alphabetical directory was introduced in 1890—hence the name, Yellow Pages. Since the 1940s, the size, scope, and usage of the Yellow Pages have grown substantially.

Advantages

This growth is attributable to the following advantages, some of which are unique to Yellow Pages advertising.

1. **Directionality.** It reaches people after they have decided to buy and guides them to a source that can satisfy their buying needs.

2. **Relative permanence.** It is published once a year and is unlikely to be discarded until the next one appears. Of course this is a major disadvantage in that once it is published the advertisements cannot be altered or updated.

3. **Consumer usage habits.** People develop the habit very early in life of looking up commercial firms in the Yellow Pages. They are used by people in all walks of life, by all income groups, and by transients as well as residents.

4. **Availability.** More than 150 million Yellow Pages directories are distributed every year, blanketing a large segment of the population. If not in every home, they are available to everyone in telephone booths, at businesses, and in other locations. They are on duty 24 hours a day, every day.

5. **Variety of advertising units.** Advertising units in the Yellow Pages range from regular listings of a firm's name, address, and telephone number to a large, attention-getting display ad. Of course, an advertiser can list under multiple classifications also.

6. **Market coverage and segmentation.** An advertiser can segment his market geographically on a city-to-city basis. Further, he can choose where in the directory he will be listed.

Guidelines: Layout

Did you know that you cannot buy a full-page ad in the Yellow Pages? This policy is to make sure there will be classified listings on every page. These listings are what builds traffic throughout the pages.

Since all Yellow Pages display ads are of a size that layout artists would regard as "small space," the standard layout recommendations and principles for all small space ads are generally observed.

1. **Keep the layout simple.** Limit the number and complexity of typography and visual elements. This avoids the clutter that discourages readership.

2. **Use white space.** White space is an important design element in advertisements. A liberal use of white space (in this instance "yellow space") will make an ad cleaner and thus easier to read and comprehend.

3. **Use recognizable visual elements.** Your objective is to gain attention to your ad and what you have to offer. If an advertiser has a distinctive logo or carries name brands, these visual elements should be featured in his Yellow Pages ad.

Guidelines: Copy

The Yellow Pages ad, because of the nature of the directory itself, is positioned among many competitors' ads. Also, space is severely restricted. This makes the copywriter's job all the more demanding. He must be succinct and to the point. No words should be wasted. And, within all these restrictions, the copy must stress those aspects of the firm that set it off from its competitors. Yellow Pages copy should follow these points:

1. **Emphasize product identification.** Vital among copy elements is the strong identification of the product or service. Repetition of this identification is recommended. Set it in type. Repeat it in the copy. Include the logo.

2. **Include brand names.** The advertiser should make it clear that he carries name brands by naming them. If he is an authorized service center or has some other differentiating characteristic, it should be specified.

3. **Emphasize line or service.** If an advertiser stocks an unusually extensive inventory or is able to perform unusual services, they should receive special mention.

4. **Give special attention to the telephone number.** Since a telephone call usually immediately follows the selection of an ad in the Yellow Pages, it makes sense to feature the telephone number.

5. **Include other vital information.** Include in the Yellow Pages ad as much information as you think is important to both the buying decision and finding the place. Included would be location, hours open, free parking, credit available, etc.

EXHIBIT **21-1.** Yellow Pages Guidelines

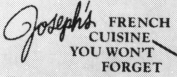

For 29 years, Joseph's has been serving fine french cuisine in an elegant atmosphere.

In those years, we've been awarded the five-star rating 11 times from the Fine Diners Club. This rating—the highest in the restaurant business—is based on the food, the service and the surroundings. We've excelled in all three categories.

Come see for yourself—we think you'd enjoy it.

JOSEPH'S
PRIVATE PARTY SPECIALISTS
SINCE 1950
100 West St. 555-1294
Open every day, 11 a.m. to 10 p.m.

THE FIVE-STAR RESTAURANT

Does your Yellow Pages ad pass the 10-point test?

1. **Headline:** *Is it a promise you can keep?*

2. **Illustration:** *Is it worth "1,000 words"?*

3. **Body copy:** *Is it convincing?*

4. **Support statement:** *Does it add authenticity?*

5. **Name and address:** *Can shoppers find you easily?*

6. **Special services:** *Do customers know why you're distinctive?*

7. **Business hours:** *Do shoppers know when you're open?*

8. **Phone number:** *Does it stand out?*

9. **Credit cards:** *Do customers know which you'll accept?*

10. **Slogan:** *Does it help people remember you?*

Stand out where smart shoppers start out

You can do a lot to beef up your Yellow Pages ad. Add a map. Run the ad in multiple classifications if more than one applies. In some directories, you can use red ink.

More than ever, it's important that your ad stand out. Because smart shoppers shop the Yellow Pages before they start out in their cars.

Yellow Pages is more than telephone numbers—it's a valuable shopping resource that can save gas, money and time.

And if that's where people start out today, that's where your advertising should stand out. In the Southwestern Bell Yellow Pages.

Southwestern Bell

SOURCE: Courtesy of Southwestern Bell. Reprinted from *Communications Update,* © 1982.

ASSIGNMENT 21-1. Writing a Yellow Pages Ad

Create a display ad for the Yellow Pages of your local telephone directory. Do copy and layout. Size: 4″ × 5″. The company, described below, is a retail operation: The A-One Brake Service.

A-One Brake Service offers complete service on all foreign and domestic cars. This includes service on wheel alignment, brakes, front end, tires, automatic transmission, air conditioning, electrical system, and exhaust system. Also: complete lubrication, complete tune-up, safety check, and computer balancing.

Telephone number: 589-6423
Address: 4205 Main Street
Service manager: Jake Wheeler

PART V
Broadcast Media

Chapter 22

Radio

Introduction

From the creative standpoint, there are some people who think radio is a relatively simple medium. However, nothing could be further from the truth. Television offers the creative person all the advantages of sight, sound, color, and motion. The TV copywriter has all these elements at his command. In radio, he has only sound to work with. Obviously, he has a more difficult task in attracting and holding the attention of his audience. The job is not easier; it's much tougher.

When a radio commercial is carefully conceived, well written, and professionally produced, however, it can undoubtedly do an effective selling job. There are many examples of highly successful campaigns in which radio was the major, and in some cases, the only medium used. With an imaginative and knowledgeable copywriter at the helm, radio can be a compelling seller of goods and services.

Advantages

In the early 1950s, because of the advent of television and other peripheral setbacks, radio entered a bleak period. But it has recovered well and is now pursuing a path of steady ascendancy. There are a number of solid reasons for its healthy condition.

Today, more than ever, radio can reach its audience just about anywhere—in the home, of course, but also in cars, trucks, and boats; at beaches and picnics; on the farm; and in factories and other places of business. Furthermore, while other media costs have risen substantially—some astronomically—in recent years, radio costs have risen more slowly and more moderately.

Radio offers great flexibility in time, geography, and audience selection, as the following list of advantages indicates.

1. While it is a disadvantage for an advertiser with a complicated sales message, audibility can be effective for mass-market products with relatively simple sales stories. No great personal effort, other than listening, is required. The homemaker cleans the house, Dad putters in the workshop, and the kids are playing in the park—while the radio is entertaining and informing and selling.

2. Like newspapers with fast closings, radio has timeliness. Radio can deliver the message *now*.

3. The development of the portable transistor has greatly increased radio ownership. Today's average household owns five radios, one for almost every room in the house.

4. Radio can put advertising dollars where the product is distributed: in local markets, through local stations, or across the country, through networks. It can work effectively for the local merchant or the chain store. It can deliver a sales message for the car dealer on automobile row or for the national advertiser.

5. Each demographic segment of the listening public can find programs to suit its interests. This ability to reach specific audiences means that radio can be selective. Young people can listen to rock and blues in their own rooms, Mom can catch a news show in the living room, and Dad can listen to a talk show in the kitchen.

6. Radio reaches commuters during "drive time"—although the advent of tape decks in cars has undoubtedly caused a decrease in radio listening in automobiles.

7. Radio can reach college students, high school students, and young people in general by appealing to their musical and, to some degree, political interests.

8. Quite a few stations have well-known disc jockeys and other personalities, whose ability to sell products can work very well for the radio advertiser.

When all these advantages, including relatively low cost, are considered, it is obvious why radio is an attractive buy for local, regional, and national advertisers.

Guidelines

Some copy guidelines may be helpful to the beginning copywriter. Here are a few.

1. **Do your homework about product and prospect.** You must do the necessary research so that you know what you're talking about. You must know your prospect, your prospect's problems, and your product in order to write your copy specifically, knowingly, and compellingly. Use both primary and secondary research to assemble facts.

2. **Open with an attention-arresting device.** Take advantage of the sound medium by using some specific audio device, particularly at the start. Examples include sound effects (Northwest Orient's gong), music (especially jingles), and unusual voices ("Hey, Culligan man"). If you don't get attention fast, you may never get it at all.

3. **Repeat your major points, especially the product identification.** As the only nonvisual medium, radio must impress points on the listener's mind by repetition. Mention your product's name early and as often as you can. Repeat other important points, such as the store's name and location and the special price or other selling points you wish to emphasize.

4. **Write conversationally.** Radio is one person talking to another. Even though it is a mass medium, radio commercials written to one person in the target market tend to be more effective. And they tend to be considerably more believable.

5. **Be succinct.** In radio, get straight to the point—and stick to it. Keep it simple. Use short sentences and short words. Not only are they more easily understood by more people, they are also more easily absorbed and remembered.

6. **Write for the eye, as well as the ear.** One of the useful characteristics of radio is that it stimulates the imagination. You can make the listener see with his mind's eye. This is a major challenge and opportunity for the creative writer.

7. **Focus on a single big idea.** In radio, it is better to concentrate on one major sales point than to try to cover several. If you inundate the listener with too much, he may retain very little. Save additional points for later commercials or other media. Use your time to get one point across.

8. **Use emphatic action words.** The active voice is always better than the passive voice. And action words are critical in effective, lively radio commercials. Use such action words as "now" and "today" and "here" and "buy." If they are appropriate, don't overlook "sale" and "free" either.

9. **Avoid humor, unless you can do it well.** Humor in radio commercials is very difficult to do effectively. In their attempt to be funny, too many writers write down to the listener and more often than not come off more ridiculous than humorous.

10. **Avoid numbers.** Because most people have trouble remembering numbers, don't use them. Instead of a street address, give a location ("Downtown on Main") or a landmark ("Just north of the high school"). Don't use telephone numbers unless they are easy to remember (474-7474). If you feel you have to use a telephone number, at least break the seven numbers into three. For instance, instead of 5-9-7-3-1-2-8, write it to be read five-ninety-seven, thirty-one, twenty-eight.

11. **Don't overdo superlatives.** Go easy on those excessive comparisons that threaten believability. If you do use one, at least be moderate, or use it with tongue in cheek. And avoid flowery, meaningless adjectives. They, too, reduce your credibility.

12. **Zero in on your audience.** Know whom you're selling to. Radio's selectivity can attract the right audience. But it's the writer's responsibility to communicate to that audience in the right language.

13. **Prepare your copy.** Underline words for emphasis. Indicate pauses clearly. Triple-space copy. If possible, make the announcer rehearse.

14. **Close big.** Don't die at the end. Close with a bang. Build throughout the commercial and hold interest until the end. Recap the major point or points in a memorable way. Ask for action.

15. **Practice your commercial out loud.** Because people read faster to themselves than out loud, be sure to time your commercial by reading it out loud. This also allows you to hear it in terms of rhythm, pace, and clarity.

Elements of Successful Radio Commercials

In its survey of radio commercials, the Yankelovich Research Company isolated eight elements that proved to be crucial in differentiating effective commercials (those that stimulate buying interest) from less effective ones. Elements to strive for and elements to avoid are given below.

Elements to Strive For

1. **Conveying meaningful content.** The listener must have the feeling that he has gotten some informational reward out of listening. This information does not have to be new or startling. It may simply reinforce what the listener already knows.

2. **Stimulating product-plus associations.** This refers to the ability of a commercial to arouse thoughts and feelings in the listener that relate to the commercial's central message.

3. **Encouraging listener identification.** Identification can be established in many ways—in a dialogue in which the product is discussed; in a straightforward presentation of the product's advantages; with music and words sung or spoken; or with sound effects.

4. **Fitting in with listener expectations.** Commercials scoring well in the results fitted in with the ideas, feelings, and images the listener already had built up about the product or service.

Elements to Avoid

1. **Offending or alienating.** A commercial should not give the listener the feeling that he is being shouted at or bullied.

2. **Eliciting suspicion and disbelief—phoniness.** This quality in a commercial reveals itself quickly to the listener.

3. **Creating confusion that distracts from the message.** When a message is unclear or incomprehensible to the listener, he loses interest (and you may lose a client to sell).

4. **Boring the listener.** Commercials that are excessively repetitive in content or difficult to understand are likely to be labeled boring or dull.

Most of the effective commercials studied by Yankelovich could be characterized as intimate and relaxed, or lively and cheerful. Whatever style or mood you select for a particular commercial message, be sure you maintain it throughout the commercial. You want the listener to come away with a definite feeling of a coherent whole. Be consistent.

Preparation of Radio Scripts

The radio script should be typed on white 8½" × 11" typing paper (or specially designed forms) and is always double-spaced. Down the left side are typed the talent and the specific audio effects, in caps (ANNOUNCER, MAN, WOMAN, NAMES, MUSIC, SOUND EFFECTS, etc.). These are typed directly across from the copy to be read or the description of the sounds or music. (See Exhibit 22-1.)

As a help to those responsible for music and sound effects, underscore music with a solid line and underscore sound effects with a broken line.

Often lines are numbered between the left and right sections to aid in referring to a particular line during rewriting or rehearsing.

The right side is devoted to the spoken copy of the talent, including the directions concerning how the words are to be spoken, and the music and sound effects. Spoken copy is typed in upper and lower case. Instructions are typed in ALL CAPITAL LETTERS (CAPS), and placed in parentheses.

For emphasis in spoken copy, underline or use caps.

Study the sample radio scripts given in Exhibits 22-2 to 22-4.

At the top of each page, type "page ____ of ____." Also, at the bottom of each page for which there is a following page, type "more." And on the last page, type "end" at the bottom.

Try to have reasons for what you do (and do not do). Explain your decisions on form and content in an accompanying "rationale" sheet, an example of which, along with the radio script it was intended to explain, is shown in Exhibit 22-5.

EXHIBIT **22-1.** *Radio Script Form*

ADVERTISER
RUN DATE
LENGTH

(LEFT SIDE OF PAGE DEVOTED TO INFO CONCERNING TALENT, SOUNDS, MUSIC, ETC., IN CAPS)	1 2 3 4 5 6	The right side of the radio script is devoted to all copy to be read, as well as directions concerning music and sound effects typed double-spaced. Underline or use CAPS for emphasis. Use (parentheses) for special instructions (SHOUT, LAUGHINGLY, ETC.). Make sure information in left column is on appropriate line to match right column.
SOUND:	7 8 9	SOUND EFFECTS ARE TYPED IN ALL CAPS AND UNDERLINED WITH BROKEN LINE. SOUND EFFECTS MAY BE LIVE OR RECORDED.
MUSIC:	10 11 12	MUSIC IS TYPED IN CAPS, UNDERLINED WITH SOLID LINE. MAY INCLUDE DIRECTIONS. GIVE RECORD NUMBER IF KNOWN, OR DESCRIBE TYPE.
ANNOUNCER:	13 14	Here are some examples of how a piece of copy might look when finished:
SOUND:	15	KNOCK ON DOOR. (PAUSE). KNOCK ON DOOR LOUDER.
INSTRUCTOR:	16	(IMPATIENTLY) Yes, what is it?
SOUND:	17	DOOR OPENING. THEN CLOSING.
COED:	18 19	Mr. Ogilvy, I'm Cathy Coed and I am flunking your course. I'll do *anything* to just pass the course.
INSTRUCTOR:	20	*Anything?*
SOUND:	21	TELEPHONE RINGS
INSTRUCTOR:	22 23	Excuse me. Hello. Yes, I can be there at noon. Good bye. Now where were we, Cathy?
COED:	24	I said I'd do *anything* to pass copy and layout.
INSTRUCTOR:	25	Then why don't you try *studying?*
MUSIC:	26	DRAGNET THEME: DUM DE DUM DUM
ANNOUNCER:	27 28	Yes, you too can pass copy and layout if you come to class, follow directions, make deadlines, work hard, and *study!*

EXHIBIT **22-2.** *Sample Radio Script*

BANK—SAVINGS DEPT.
60 seconds

ANNOUNCER:	1	The nickel is an interesting sort of coin. It's larger, heavier, and a
	2	good deal more impressive looking than a dime. It'll buy five times
	3	as much as your average penny. And it has a distinctive "plink" all
	4	its own when dropped, thus . . .
SOUND:	5	COIN DROPPING
ANNOUNCER	6	. . . when you deposit a dollar in a (ADVERTISER) savings account,
	7	at the end of a year we'll give you back a dollar *and* a nickel. That's
	8	a dollar five for every dollar you save. In bank terms that's a
	9	payment of five percent on your dollar, the highest interest in
	10	(STATE). Now, you may think a year's a long time to wait around
	11	for a little nickel . . .
SOUND:	12	COIN DROPPING
ANNOUNCER:	13	. . . but if you bring us, say, a thousand dollars, that's a thousand
	14	nickels . . .
SOUND:	15	MANY COINS DROPPING
ANNOUNCER:	16	. . . and that's not bad at all. (ADVERTISER), Member FDIC.

TARGET: Men and women
TECHNIQUE: Straight announce/sound
THEME: Customer advantage

ANALYSIS: Imaginative use of sound makes savings appreciation very tangible. In this example, it's used first to portray a single coin and then to make the multiplication into a thousand vividly real. It's probably well worth the extra trouble to think out such uses of sound, for the result will be a commercial of superior effectiveness.

EXHIBIT **22-3.** *Sample Radio Script*

INFANT WEAR STORE
30 seconds

SOUND:	1	BABY'S GURGLE
ANNOUNCER:	2	That's the sound of an authority. Little girls and little guys don't
	3	know much about size, but they do know when they're comfortable.
	4	That's why wise parents shop at the (ADVERTISER). They know
	5	that comfort comes first at the (ADVERTISER). It's where you'll find
	6	the best buys in quality, value, and cozy comfort. But don't take our
	7	word for it. Ask an authority . . .
SOUND:	8	BABY'S GURGLE
ANNOUNCER:	9	The (ADVERTISER). (ADDRESS)

TARGET: Mothers
TECHNIQUE: Straight announce/sound
THEME: Image

ANALYSIS: The baby is an unimpeachable authority, whose "testimonial" few would dare question. The same approach has been used for years for baby foods, diapers, laundry products, etc. It is applicable, also, to infant furniture, baby carriages, home heating and air conditioning, floor covering, or anything with which an infant might be involved.

EXHIBIT **22-4.** *Sample Radio Script*

LAWN AND GARDEN STORE
60 seconds

ANNOUNCER:	1	The (ADVERTISER) story lives on.
MUSIC:	2	
ANNOUNCER:	3	(ADVERTISER) is a hammer that won't strike your thumb.
MUSIC:	4	
MAN:	5	(ADVERTISER) is a gallon of paint that won't peel.
MUSIC	6	
WOMAN:	7	(ADVERTISER) is a kitchen cabinet that's never full.
MUSIC	8	
MAN:	9	(ADVERTISER) is a nail that never bends.
MUSIC:	10	
MAN:	11	(ADVERTISER) is a lawn that grows green.
MUSIC:	12	
MAN:	13	(ADVERTISER) is an outdoor barbecue.
MUSIC:	14	
WOMAN:	15	(ADVERTISER) is low prices and warm service.
ANNOUNCER:	16	Come, listen to the warm. (ADVERTISER) has it all for you, your
	17	home, and your garden. (ADVERTISER.) (ADDRESS.)

TARGET: Men and women home owners
TECHNIQUE: Straight announce/sound
THEME: Customer advantage

ANALYSIS: This is a brief shopping list approach. It has been used successfully for many kinds of retailers. In this case, it is combined with a testimonial implication, stressing particular customer advantages for both men and women. The brevity of the spot, in terms of ground covered, permits a whole series of similar commercials, featuring different products and services. The same approach might work well for a department store, variety store, drug store, etc.

EXHIBIT 22-5. Rationale and Radio Script

The following rationale was provided by Ayres and Associates, Inc., Lincoln, Nebraska, for its client, Mickelberry Meats.

Mickelberry :30 Radio Commercial—"Rubber Hot Dog"

This script is part of a campaign that won an Andy Award of Distinction from the Advertising Club of New York and a prestigious Clio recognition. All for an unknown meat packer in rural Nebraska. This commercial is proof that success is not limited to big clients, nor creativity to lavish budgets.

Because the Mickelberry brand was a relative unknown, even in its home markets, we wanted a high-profile, high-recognition format that would primarily build brand awareness while giving us an opportunity to stress good taste and quality. We found it in a humorous interview format that gave us an opportunity to play with our product and give our listeners the chance to see our half-minute plays in their imagination.

This approach has its roots in the Stan Freberg school of radio advertising. It's sort of like doing television without a television budget. In fact, when listeners were interviewed about the Mickelberry spots, many gave full and vivid descriptions of characters and situations. Just as if they had seen the commercials on television. This campaign went on to become an unqualified success in every market in which it was placed.

MICKELBERRY MEATS
30 seconds

1st MAN:	This is your Mickelberry man on the street, and today's question is: "Would you eat a rubber hot dog?" Excuse me.
2nd MAN:	Yes?
1st MAN:	Sir . . . ?
2nd MAN:	Umm-hm?
1st MAN:	Would you eat a rubber hot dog?
2nd MAN:	A *rubber* hot dog?
1st MAN:	Take your time . . . think about it.
2nd MAN:	Aaaah—NO!
1st MAN:	Would you eat this plump and juicy Mickelberry hot dog?
2nd MAN:	Sure, uh-huh.
1st MAN:	Go ahead. Now, you say the *Mickelberry* hot dog is *better* than the rubber hot dog?
2nd MAN:	The rubber hot dog is the one I *wouldn't* eat?
1st MAN:	Yes.
2nd MAN:	This is much better.
1st MAN:	Oh good. That proves it. *Mickelberry* hot dogs are *better* than rubber hot dogs.
2nd MAN:	Much better!
1st MAN:	Thank you.

Timing Simple Commercials

The time of a radio commercial is vital. It should be very close to the designated time, whether 10, 20, 30, or 60 seconds. The most accurate (and ultimately the best) method of timing commercials is just to time them. But while you are writing on a typewriter, it is helpful to know how much time you have used as you go along. The form in Exhibit 22-7 is designed for that purpose.

The form is lined for several lengths of commercials. By typing within the specified lines, you can estimate a commercial's time with considerable accuracy. The form is lined for a width of 50 characters (see Exhibit 22-6), but you could convert the system to other widths with a little calculation and experimentation. For instance, 20 lines of 50 characters (60-seconds) would convert to about 16½ lines of 60 characters. Simply divide 1,000 characters by the character width. For 50-character lines, the time translates to about three seconds per line.

This system works best for single-voice, straight-delivery commercials. It *might* work for other approaches, such as multiple voices, and commercials with music, sound effects, many numbers, and so on, but it is not likely to since each additional voice or sound takes up more time.

EXHIBIT **22-6.** **Determining Character Widths**

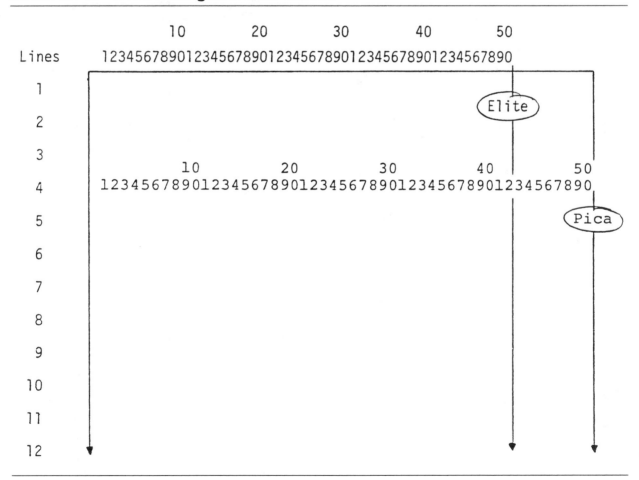

EXHIBIT **22-7.**   Timing Form for Simple Radio Commercials

1. Select line width for typewriter—elite or pica.
2. Select line limit for number of lines (according to desired time).
3. Type within those lines as much as possible. (Lines going over width will balance out short lines.)
4. Always time after writing, reading aloud.

	Elite	Pica
1.		
2.		
3.		
4.		10 seconds
5.		
6.		
7.		20 seconds
8.		
9.		
10.		30 seconds
11.		
12.		
13.		
14.		
15.		
16.		
17.		
18.		
19.		
20.		60 seconds

EXHIBIT **22-8.** *Radio Checklist and Evaluation*

	Very Good	Good	Fair	Weak	Very Weak
RATIONALE:					
1. Prospect analysis	[ ]	[ ]	[ ]	[ ]	[ ]
2. Advertisement analysis	[ ]	[ ]	[ ]	[ ]	[ ]
CONTENT:					
1. Product identification	[ ]	[ ]	[ ]	[ ]	[ ]
2. Attention-arresting device	[ ]	[ ]	[ ]	[ ]	[ ]
3. Simple, clear	[ ]	[ ]	[ ]	[ ]	[ ]
4. Reads smoothly	[ ]	[ ]	[ ]	[ ]	[ ]
5. Focuses on single big idea	[ ]	[ ]	[ ]	[ ]	[ ]
6. Suited for client	[ ]	[ ]	[ ]	[ ]	[ ]
7. Creative, fresh, clever	[ ]	[ ]	[ ]	[ ]	[ ]
8. Use of radio (music, sound effects)	[ ]	[ ]	[ ]	[ ]	[ ]
9. Strong close	[ ]	[ ]	[ ]	[ ]	[ ]
MISCELLANEOUS:					
1. Mechanics					
A. Times out OK?	[ ]	[ ]	[ ]	[ ]	[ ]
B. Form correct?	[ ]	[ ]	[ ]	[ ]	[ ]
2. Overall idea and ad	[ ]	[ ]	[ ]	[ ]	[ ]
3. Spelling and grammar	[ ]	[ ]	[ ]	[ ]	[ ]
4. Followed directions (on time, etc.)	[ ]	[ ]	[ ]	[ ]	[ ]

COMMENTS:

ASSIGNMENT **22-1.** Writing a Radio Commercial

Write a 60-second radio commercial aimed at the audience described below, promoting horse-betting as a socially acceptable activity and Penguin Raceway as a respectable place to visit.

Write a 30-second spinoff.

Production Note: Music and sound effects may be used.

Penguin Raceway is a successful enterprise featuring harness racing. It is located on the outskirts of a midwestern city. The track has just been purchased by an aggressive, promotion-minded owner who feels that while attendance has been good, it can be better with effective promotion on radio and TV.

His goal is to attract a more diversified patronage, including reputable and cultured people in the upper-middle-income bracket, women, and married couples.

He feels that the way to accomplish this goal is to play up the aesthetic aspects of the track: the beauty of the plant, the luxury and decoration of the restaurant and public areas, the attractiveness of the landscaping, and the vivid beauty of the horses.

Additional features: excellent dining, convenient parking and betting facilities, fine quality horses and famous jockeys. Other features: easy accessibility from the city, courteous attendants and window clerks, and a new, free bus service from the parking lot to the stands. All in all, this is a track designed for the patron's total comfort and enjoyment.

ASSIGNMENT **22-2.** Writing a Radio Commercial

Write a 60-second spot for the restaurant described below, using only an announcer. Then write a 60-second spot, using two or more voices, plus music and sound effects.

A new sea food restaurant will be opening in a medium-sized southwestern city. It will be the first and only restaurant that features only fish on the menu. Fresh fish, delivered fresh every day. Fresh shrimp and scallops. Ocean-fresh perch. Tender fillet of haddock. Lobster. Lobster tails. Clams and oysters. Opening day special is free coffee and dessert, home-made apple pie, with every meal.

It should be emphasized that this is the first and only establishment in town with such a wide variety of sea food—all fresh. Guaranteed fresh.

ASSIGNMENT **22-3.** *Writing a Radio Commercial*

Write a 60-second radio spot for the tennis club described below. You may use whatever talent you deem suitable, as well as music and sound effects.

Do a 30-second spinoff.

> A local indoor tennis club has expanded its facilities and now offers a new fitness program. Designed for total body fitness and cardiovascular endurance, it is called the "Sunrise Stretch," for singles or couples over 50. Sessions start with stretching, jumping, light jogging, and exercises. They end with yoga and relaxation techniques. Topped with a free breakfast. Mondays, Wednesdays, Fridays from 7:30 to 8:15 A.M. twelve sessions only $29.50 for singles, $49.00 for couples (includes breakfast).

Chapter 23

Television

Introduction

Television advertising is powerful. Combining both visual and audio appeal, it can be more arresting than any other advertising medium. Even commercial-hating critics agree about that. It has sight, sound, movement, color, and an open invitation to enter the homes of millions of viewers. Average TV viewing time in the home is 6½ hours a day.

But unless TV advertising is entirely believable—consistently believable—its power as a medium to persuade and to sell will soon evaporate. And believability comes only from the elimination of anything potentially misleading, or even confusing, unintentional though it may be. There is little doubt however, that some commercials do exaggerate and perhaps even bend the truth a bit. When this happens, doubt is cast on all the others and, indeed, on all advertisements in all media.

Advantages

Television is an effective advertising medium for many reasons. Some of its advantages over other media are given below. It should be emphasized, however, that TV's most attractive attribute is that it is watched by so many, so often, and for so long.

Impact

Television is both audible (like radio) and visible (like print). Furthermore, its visual materials are in motion. And by combining spoken copy and moving pictures, it can produce sales messages forcefully and compellingly. The fact that TV sights and sounds are more lifelike than they are in any other medium gives a credibility to its creations that other media cannot match. People tend to believe what they can see with their own eyes, and television is the only medium that can actually put before the public's eyes what the product looks like in real life, how it is used, and how people feel about it when they use it.

Selectivity

Television is America's favorite entertainment medium. It can reach any age group and any demographic segment. Commercials can be spotted on after-school programs designed for children, on daytime dramas directed at housewives, and on nighttime sports shows that attract adult male viewers. Spot TV affords both the chain store and the national advertiser an opportunity to put their promotional efforts into markets where sales potential is greatest or where a store or a product needs bolstering.

Flexibility

Time on television can be purchased locally, regionally, and nationally, so it can be utilized by both local and national advertisers. Independent retailers can use local TV production facilities at relatively low cost. Most local stations have creative and production people capable of producing effective commercials.

Guidelines

How can a TV spot be legal, clean, honest, and truthful and still be imaginative, dramatic, memorable, competitive, daring, hard hitting, and persuasive—and accomplish all that in 60 or, most frequently, 30 seconds?

It's not easy. Yet it is done with surprising consistency. There's no magic formula for reaching the creative heights in a TV spot, but here are some basic guidelines to follow:

1. **Do your homework.** All media advertising should begin with research, and television is no exception. Get all the facts about your prospect, your prospect's problems, and your product or service before you even pick up a pencil to write.

2. **Select your strongest selling point or benefit.** Analyze, then crystallize your research into major and minor selling points (product points) and benefits (prospect points). Then focus on the strongest, most provocative possibility for a selling idea, and stress it.

3. **Make your proposition relevant.** Your commercial should be relevant to the viewer's wants and needs. Make your proposition meaningful to him, in his terms. Tell him what's in it for him.

4. **Assume your prospect is intelligent.** Along with your native imagination and creativity, use taste, discretion, and respect for your prospect's intelligence. As David Ogilvy once said, "The consumer is not stupid. She is your wife."

5. **Open strong.** The opening seconds of your commercial are vital. Although we could speak of grabbing attention, it would probably be more accurate to speak of "holding" the attention already attracted by the program. In either case, it is critical to prevent the viewer from taking a commercial break, either mentally or physically.

6. **Keep your commercial on target.** While you are creating your commercial, check back frequently with your copy platform. Stay on the track. Too often the writer gets sidetracked and wrapped up in being clever and forgets the primary goal—to communicate.

7. **Use an appropriate technique.** Whatever technique you use for your commercial, it should be compatible with the product or service and the image you wish to project. You can destroy a good idea with the wrong technique.

8. **Take advantage of the visual opportunities.** Since television is primarily a visual medium, use it to best advantage. Show your product. Demonstrate it. Make your video carry more than half the weight of the message. Avoid long, static scenes. Provide for movement.

9. **Make every word count.** Don't waste words. Usually you have only 30 seconds to say what you have to say. Consider each one carefully. Make each one contribute to the message.

10. **Coordinate audio and video.** The audio and video must relate to each other throughout your commercial. If they don't, confusion will result and neither the eye nor the ear will understand what you're trying to say. Which comes first, words or pictures? It depends on your creativity, but try it both ways.

11. **Write conversational copy.** Television has been compared to the personal salesman in that it creates a person-to-person, almost face-to-face selling situation. This suggests that you should write your copy in a natural, conversational tone. Avoid the pretentious, the glib, the false manner.

12. **Don't worry about art.** When you are creating your storyboard, don't worry about your lack of artistic ability. Drawings can be simple. Try to be as specific as possible, to help the artist, but stick figures and rough sketches are acceptable.

13. **Emphasize product identification.** A major failure of most television commercials is that they do not clearly or strongly register product identification. Above all else, make sure you have identified your brand clearly and forcefully.

14. **Consider the announcement approach.** If your product (or service) is new or has a new feature, give your spot an announcement flavor. Television viewers, like newspaper readers, look for, appreciate, and react favorably to new things.

15. **Repeat your major points.** Repetition can help register a selling idea. Don't expect the viewer to remember it if you say it or show it only once in your commercial. Remember the old adage, ''Tell them what you're going to tell them, tell them, and then tell them what you told them.''

16. **Involve your prospect emotionally.** Even though you may have used some gimmick or mechanical technique to attract attention to your commercial, don't lose sight of the fact that you must keep that attention. Appealing to basic human wants and needs will help to maintain interest and develop it into desire that leads to action.

17. **Time your commercial carefully.** Obviously your commercial must time out accurately. But don't rely on reading it to yourself. Read it aloud. Act it out; walk through it. A pace too fast will leave the viewer far behind. Don't rush it.

18. **Reconsider your finished script.** Once you are satisfied with your script, set it aside. Reconsider it later as objectively as you can. Examine it for impact, clarity, rhythm, pace, persuasion, relevance,

believability. Submit it to others for their evaluation. If it does not score high—revise it.

19. **Don't be afraid to start over.** If, during the creating of the script or storyboard you think of a better way to do it, or are unhappy with the way things are going, start over. Don't be too proud to begin again.

20. **Rewrite and then rewrite again.** Don't expect to write a final script or storyboard on the first try. True professionals rewrite and polish through many versions, up to the last minute.

Preparation of TV Scripts and Storyboards

The unique character of television—embodying both sight and sound—demands that creative work be very carefully prepared. Sometimes TV commercials require only a script. Sometimes they require only a storyboard. Occasionally, they require both. You will be instructed as to which ones are needed for any given assignment. As always, identify the advertiser, the medium, and the details of scheduling in the upper left-hand corner of the page.

Scripts

TV scripts are to be typed on white 8½" × 11" typing paper. The left third of the page, devoted to video, is double-spaced and typed in capital letters. The right two-thirds of the page, devoted to audio, is also double-spaced, but is typed in upper and lower case. Audio *instructions,* however, are typed in caps.

Do not hyphenate words at the ends of lines. Number each scene. Line up video instructions with corresponding audio instructions. (See Exhibit 23-1.) Study and follow the style of the sample scripts in Exhibits 23-2 and 23-3. At the bottom of each page, indicate that there is another page by typing "more." On the final page, type "end."

Storyboards

A storyboard is a combination of the written material from a script and rough sketches of key frames showing what is described in the video. There are several commercial storyboard forms available, one of which is shown in Exhibit 23-4. Photocopy or trace additional sheets as needed.

Number each frame in order. Sketch what is seen in key scenes in each frame. Be accurate, and make your sketches as detailed as possible. Stick figures are permitted. Do not paste illustrations onto the storyboard.

Under each frame, type the video and audio exactly as you would on a script, but single-space video in caps and double-space audio in upper and lower case. Do not mount storyboards unless instructed to do so. Indicate page numbers in the upper right-hand corner: "page ____ of ____." Use the video directions described in Exhibit 23-5 and study the storyboards shown in Exhibits 23-6 to 23-8.

As with scripts, type "more" at the bottom of each page after which there is an additional page. On the last page, type "end."

Provide an explanation for your script and storyboard in a "rationale" sheet accompanying your finished work. Examples (and the storyboards they explain) are shown in Exhibits 23-7 and 23-8.

EXHIBIT **23-1.** Television Script Form

ADVERTISER
RUN DATE
LENGTH

VIDEO	AUDIO
DESCRIPTION OF WHAT IS SHOWN ON THE SCREEN IS TYPED ON LEFT ⅓ OF PAGE, SINGLE-SPACED IN CAPS.	Copy for what is heard is typed on the right ⅔ of the page, upper and lower case, double-spaced. Underline or use CAPS for emphasis. Any special instructions are put in CAPS and in (PARENTHESES).
1. NUMBER EACH SCENE AND MAKE SURE IT IS LINED UP DIRECTLY ACROSS FROM THE AUDIO THAT GOES WITH IT.	OLD MAN (DISGUSTEDLY): What da ya mean by that?
2. WHEN USING FILM, SAY IF IT IS SOUND-ON-FILM AND DESIGNATE SOF. PUT SOF SYMBOL ON AUDIO SIDE ALSO. INDICATE THUS:	CHILD (EXCITEDLY): Mom! Look, Mom! No cavities!
	Indicate after talent whether to be (ON CAMERA) or (VOICE OVER), which can be abbreviated (VO).
3. ROLL FILM, R27-3, SOF	ANNCR: (VO) Here at last, ladies, is . . .
4. WHEN USING SLIDES, USE "SLIDE" OR "SL" AND GIVE DESCRIPTION, THUS:	Music should be cued and underlined, as follows:
	MUSIC: IN
	MUSIC: OUT
5. TAKE SLIDE, TWO BOYS ON TEETER-TOTTER, (OR)	MUSIC: IN AND UNDER ON CUE
6. SLIDE 23D, MALE STUDENT STUDYING IN LIBRARY.	MUSIC: UP AND HOLD UNTIL END
7. WHEN LIVE STUDIO, DESCRIBE THE SCENE HERE. INDICATE A "TAKE" (DIRECT VIDEO TRANSITION) OR A "DISSOLVE" (A SLOW VIDEO FADE-OUT OF ONE SHOT AND A FADE-IN OF ANOTHER).	Sound effects should be indicated with the word "SOUND" or "SFX" and underlined with broken line:
	SOUND: DOORBELL RING
	SFX: DOG BARKING
8. SOME TERMS TO USE TO INDICATE SCREEN COMPOSITION.	When sound on the filmtrack (SOF) is used, include the final sentence in the audio as a cue to the talent.
WS: WIDE SHOT MS: MEDIUM SHOT or MCU CU: CLOSE-UP BCU: BIG CLOSE-UP ECU: EXTREME CLOSE-UP	Help all people concerned—director, cameraman, talent, and client—understand both the audio and video and how they are related.

EXHIBIT **23-2.** Sample Television Script

U.S. NAVY   page 1 of 2
PUBLIC SERVICE
60 SECONDS

VIDEO	AUDIO
1. OPEN WITH CAMERA MOUNTED IN NOSE OF PLANE AS IT WEAVES IN AND OUT OF CLOUDS, SOARS STRAIGHT UP AT SUN, THEN DIVES BACK THROUGH CLOUDS.	SOUND: MUSIC UP FOR THREE BARS, THEN DOWN AND HOLD UNDER. ANNCR: (VO) For thousands of years, the sunlight . . .
2. PLANE BURSTS THROUGH CLOUDS AND CONTINUES DIVE TOWARD SEA FAR BELOW.	. . . and the sea and the masterless winds have met in lonely rendezvous.
3. SEA SEEMS TO RUSH UP AT PLANE AS DESCENT CONTINUES.	Man did not dare venture in the endless stream that flowed forever.
4. DISSOLVE TO SHOT OF OCEAN AS AIRPLANE SKIMS TOPS OF WAVES (WIDE ANGLE LENS)	The sea was the end of earth . . . the beginning of heaven.
5. CROSS DISSOLVE TO CLOSE SHOT OF RAGING STORM, HUGE WAVES.	Boundless . . . infinite. Awesome and terrible in its mindless fury.
6. DISSOLVE TO LONELY SEAGULL SILHOUETTED AGAINST SKY.	SOUND: RAUCOUS CRY OF SEAGULL ANNCR: But then came the adventurers and the bold ones . . . who sailed forth in frail craft to defy the unkown vastness.
7. PAN UP TO HUGE MOON, THEN TO RAYS OF MOON ON WATER.	Hardy men who steered by the sun, moon and stars.
8. CUT TO MLS FROZEN WATERS IN ARCTIC. LARGE ICEBERG IN FG.	To the north . . a world of ice.
9. CUT TO MLS OF SHORE AS SEEN FROM SEA. INCLUDE TREES, ETC.	To the west . . . green and fertile countries.

U.S. NAVY   page 2 of 2

VIDEO	AUDIO
10. DS TO TWO BODIES OF WATER, LINKED BY NARROW BRIDGE OF EARTH OR SAND. WAVES CRASH THROUGH, BRIDGE DISSOLVES AND TWO BODIES OF WATER MERGE.	And in time . . . all the lands of the world were linked by the seas. MUSIC: GRADUALLY BUILDS
11. DS TO CLOSE SHOT OF WATER AS IT COVERS SAND OF SHORE, THEN RECEDES. AS ACTION IS REPEATED, DOLLY IN FOR CLOSER SHOT OF SAND.	ANNCR: And it is in this tradition of a distant and heroic past . . . of countless centuries . . . and numberless voyages . . . MUSIC: UP STRONG
12. CUT TO OVER THE SHOULDER SHOT OF SAILOR ON DESTROYER (TWILIGHT, SUN SINKING)	ANNCR: that the men of the United States Navy . . .
13. CUT TO ECU OF BOW AS IT CUTS THROUGH WATER.	. . . sail the seas today. MUSIC: UP AND OUT.

#   #   #

EXHIBIT **23-3.** Sample Television Script

KELLOGG CO.
30-sec. film
"PUTT-PUTT BOAT"
RAISIN BRAN

VIDEO	AUDIO
1. MCU OF TUGBOAT WHOOSHING PAST CAMERA. ZOOM BACK:	SOUND: BOATSWAIN'S WHISTLE
	ANNCR: (VO) (DRAMATICALLY) Now get this . . .
	SOUND: PUTT-PUTTING OF BOAT
2. TO SHOW TUGBOAT MOVING IN TUB. BOY WITH SAILOR HAT IN BIG GRIN.	ANNCR: (VO) Now get this . . . New Putt-Putt, the toy tugboat from Kellogg's Raisin Bran. New Putt-Putt skims across the water . . .
3. ANGLE CU OF TUGBOAT SHOWING HOW AIR SHOOTS OUT AND PROPELS IT.	SOUND: PUTT-PUTTING
	ANNCR: (VO) . . . powered by jet-air, from a balloon.
4. TILT UP TO SHOW BALLOON. BOAT PASSES OUT OF FRAME.	SOUND: BOATSWAIN'S WHISTLE
	ANNCR: (VO) Now hear this . . . you get this Putt-Putt tugboat, plus special balloon for only twenty-five cents . . .
5. CU OF BLURB ON FRONT OF RAISIN BRAN PACKAGE.	. . . and one boxtop from
6. ZOOM BACK FOR FULL SHOT.	. . . Kellogg's Raisin Bran. Look for this special offer . . .
7. PKG. FLIPS TO SHOW BACK.	. . . on the back of Kellogg's Raisin Bran packages and clear the deck . . .
8. ZOOM TO CU OF TUGBOAT.	. . . for smooth sailing!
	SOUND: PUTT-PUTTING

EXHIBIT **23-4.** TV Storyboard Form

EXHIBIT **23-5.** *Video Directions*

Angle shot. A camera shot taken from any position except straight on.

Close-up. A camera shot that shows the actors' faces.

Crawl. Graphics (usually credit copy) that move slowly up the screen.

Cut. An instantaneous transition from one scene to another.

Dissolve. The fade-in of a new scene over the fade-out of a previous one.

Dolly (in or out). A slow frame change accomplished by moving the camera forward or backward.

ECU (extreme close-up). Shows the actors' features.

Follow shot. The camera follows the movement of the subject without moving itself.

Freeze frame. The technique of holding a particular frame still on screen for a desired length of time.

Full shot. The actors and entire background scene are in frame.

MCU (medium close-up). The actors are seen waist-up.

MS (medium shot). The actors' whole bodies are in frame.

O.C. (on camera). Someone visible is speaking.

Over the shoulder shot. A camera shot of a performer from across the shoulder of the character to whom he is speaking.

Pan (left or right). Camera movement from a set position, along a horizontal arc.

Tilt (up or down). Camera movement from a set position, along a vertical arc.

Truck. A slow frame change accomplished by moving the camera sideways.

V.O. (voice-over). Someone invisible is speaking.

Whip shot. A fast pan shot, blurring the action on the screen.

Wipe. An optical effect in which a line or object appears to move across the screen, revealing a new picture.

Zoom. Move in or out very quickly.

ECU (extreme close-up). When used to describe a shot of a person, the camera would reveal *only the individual's head*.

When used to describe a shot of an inanimate object, the camera would fill the screen with the product.

CU (close-up). When used to describe a shot of a person, the camera would reveal the individual's *head and shoulders*.

When used to describe a shot of an inanimate object, the camera would frame the item so that some blank area around it is visible.

Tight MCU (tight medium close-up). When used to describe a shot of a person, the camera would reveal the individual *from head to chest*.

When used to describe an inanimate object, the camera would frame the item, as well as additional accessories.

EXHIBIT **23-5.** Video Directions (continued)

MCU (medium close-up). When used to describe a shot of a person, the camera would frame the individual *from head to waist.*

When used to describe a shot of an inanimate object, the camera would frame the object, as well as the foreground, background and accessories on the sides of the screen.

Loose MCU. When used to describe a shot of a person, the camera would frame the individual *from head to hips* or slightly below ¾ length of the jacket. This shot is not used on inanimate objects.

MSL (medium long shot). When used to describe a shot of a person, the camera would frame the individual *from head to knees* or slightly below hem length. This camera shot should not be used on inanimate objects alone. It may be used when a person is with the object. Example: MLS/ Announcer & refrigerator, not MLS/Refrigerator.

LS (long shot). When used to describe a shot of a person, the camera would frame the individual *from head to toes.* Do not use this on inanimate objects alone. It may be used when a person is with the object. Example: LS/Announcer & refrigerator. *Not* LS/Refrigerator. In this case the proper instruction is "COVER" (see definition).

ELS (extreme long shot). When used to describe a shot of a person, the camera would frame the individual *from head to toes* with plenty of foreground and headroom showing in the picture.

Normally this shot would not be used on inanimate objects except in rare cases when a dramatic effect is desirable (as shown in the sketch) or when the item is part of a large set. For example, a refrigerator in a kitchen setup.

Cover. This shot is usually used only on large inanimate objects or when the announcer is part of a large set, such as a kitchen or living room. Generally, a cover shot means the camera frames the item or display so that all portions of it are visible. For example: Cover shot of sofa, cover shot of a mass coffee table display, cover shot of a refrigerator. The term "Cover" is *not* used for small items, such as packages or containers. In these cases the terms CU and MCU should be used.

EXHIBIT **23-6.** Rationale and TV Storyboard

The following rationale was provided by Ayres and Associates, Inc., Lincoln, Nebraska, for its client, Mickelberry Meats.

Mickelberry :30 Television Commercial—"Bread"

"Bread" was created for Mickelberry Meats, a relatively unknown brand in its markets. The spot was designed to be highly visible in a memorable and amusing manner. Because of the client's lower budget, the agency elected to make one memorable, more expensive commercial, rather than several less expensive ones. "Bread" was targeted toward families with wives 18–34 and two or more children ages 6–12.

MCU OF ANNOUNCER SITTING.
ZOOM BACK

ANNCR: We're talking about Mickelberry meats with a loaf of bread. Tell us how it all began.

TO SHOW ANNOUNCER SITTING IN FRONT OF LARGE SCREEN WITH LOAF OF BREAD.

BREAD: I was a crumb. I didn't have the crust to slice it.

BREAD: I squandered my dough.

ANNOUNCER GESTURES AND ASKS:

ANNCR: Then you found Mickelberry?

The primary objective was brand name awareness, with perceived quality, good taste, and variety as secondary objectives. Animation was chosen to give Mickelberry a personality that would stand out from competitive brands, and the characters were created to fit the humorous format already established in an award-winning radio series.

In the beginning, we considered bringing the radio series to television, but decided not to do so. It was felt that the humorous radio vignettes played much better in the listeners' imaginations than in actual viewing. As an answer to a humorous interview that would play well on television, we created commercials with absurd characters, rather than absurd actions.

BREAD ANSWERS

BREAD: Yes, Mickelberry pickle loaf, Mickelberry bologna, all-beef franks . . . all 28 varieties. They gave me the strength to rise above the ordinary to become a Mickelberry sandwich.

ANNOUNCER ASKS QUESTION, BREAD ANSWERS

ANNCR: And now?

BREAD: I'm in loaf! I don't need the dough. I have Mickelberry.

CLOSE-UP OF ANNOUNCER

ANNCR: Those puns are awful. You must be crazy.

LS OF ANNOUNCER AND SCREEN, ENDING WITH SUPER "MICKELBERRY MEATS . . . A COLD CUT ABOVE."

BREAD: You're the one who's talking to a loaf of bread.

VO: Mickelberry Meats, a cold cut above.

EXHIBIT **23-7.** Rationale and TV Storyboard

Austin Humane Society :30 Television Commercial—"Crying Boy"

The Humane Society of Austin & Travis County (Texas) approached the Department of Advertising at the University of Texas to produce a television commercial as a public service. With an ever-increasing pet population at the pound, and rapidly increasing costs in housing and caring for pets, the Society was interested in trying to encourage people to neuter their pets so they couldn't have offspring.

The selected student-produced commercial took a "sympathy" approach. The objective was to show the sad situation when puppies are not wanted or cannot be kept and are taken to the pound. The viewer feels sorry for both the boy and the unwanted puppies. Most people will think ahead to

CU OF CHILD'S WAGON WITH PUPPIES IN IT. SIGN ON WAGON SAYS "PUPPIES FOR SALE, 50¢." CAMERA ZOOMS BACK . . .

SOUND: PUPPY SQUEALS, FOLLOWED BY KNOCKS ON DOOR.

. . . TO SHOW YOUNG BOY AT DOOR OF HOUSE. WOMAN OPENS DOOR AND STEPS FORWARD.

WOMAN: Good morning!

BOY: Would you like to buy a puppy? They're only fifty cents.

WOMAN SHAKES HER HEAD "NO."

CU OF WAGON SHOWING SIGN WITH THE "50¢" CROSSED OUT AND NEW PRICE OF "25¢" WRITTEN IN.

what might happen to the puppies at the pound if they are not adopted (they are put to sleep if not adopted or claimed in a certain time).

The line in the commercial "You pay for them, one way or another" refers to the tax dollars used to help support the Society. The closing line is the objective of the commercial: "Neuter your pet. It's the only humane thing to do."

In addition to the primary message (to neuter pets in order to hold down pet populations), the commercial was intended to build awareness of the Humane Society and its problems. Hopefully, the public would give support to the organization in the form of money donations during the next fund-raising campaign.

PULL BACK TO SHOW BOY HOLDING PUPPY AS HE TALKS TO MAN WATERING HIS LAWN.

BOY: Would you like to buy a puppy, mister?

MAN: No, I don't want one.

CUT TO UNIFORMED MAN FROM HUMANE SOCIETY PUTTING PUPPIES IN HIS TRUCK AND CLOSING DOOR AS SAD BOY WATCHES.

ANNCR: (VO) There's no excuse for unwanted pets.

SUPER: "THE HUMANE SOCIETY OF AUSTIN, 478-0000," ON SCENE AS TRUCK DRIVES OFF, BOY WATCHES.

ANNCR: (VO) You pay for them, one way or another.

DISSOLVE TO CU OF BOY CRYING, THEN WIPES A TEAR FROM HIS EYE.

ANNCR: (VO) Neuter your pet. It's the only humane thing to do.

EXHIBIT **23-8.** TV Storyboards

Television commercials, 30 and 60 seconds long, provide ample opportunity for showing a variety of product applications and service offerings. The presentation can be highly dramatic, surrealistic, or straightforward.

(Singers) Alcoa can't wait.
(Anncr.) Take a look at
aluminum...flying.

Aluminum...trucking.

Aluminum...jet foiling.

Aluminum is reducing
weight and saving energy.

Because the lighter
something is, the less
fuel it takes to move it.

Aluminum! It's the metal
that moves America.

And we're doing it now!

(Singers) Alcoa can't wait.
(Anncr.) We can't wait
for tomorrow.

1. (MUSIC)

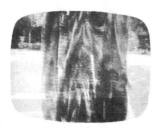

2. (MUSIC)

3. WOMAN: I am made of blue
sky

4. and golden light.

5. And I will feel this way
forever.

6. (MUSIC)

7. ANNCR: Share the fantasy.

8. Chanel Number 5.

Product demonstrations are particularly effective in TV commercials. They can create maximum viewer identification and communicate maximum product information. They can appeal to any emotion, from love and joy to frustration and sorrow.

BOY: Ladies and gentlemen. For my first trick...

CHORUS SINGS: So different and so new,

was like any other...

(SFX) until we saw you, make it happen.

ANNCR: (VO) Introduce your child to The Fisher-Price Magic Show.

Fifteen magic tricks... especially made for kids.

GIRL: Its magic, Grandma! GRANDMA: Oh, Susie, it sure is!

ANNCR: (VO) The Magic Show. By Fisher-Price.

SFX: MUSIC UNDER THROUGHOUT. WOMAN: I gotta lose weight. I gotta lose weight.

ANNCR (VO): There you sit ... skipping meals to lose weight.

WOMAN: I gotta lose weight. ANNCR (VO): But skipping meals isn't smart. Nutrition's too important.

ANNCR (VO): So skip with Figurines. Two Figurines bars provide the nutrition of a sensible meal,

without the meal. So in your diet plan, Figurines helps you lose weight.

WOMAN: I'm gonna lose weight ... I'm gonna lose weight.

ANNCR (VO): When you skip that fattening meal ... Don't skip nutrition.

Skip with Figurines!

SOURCES: Courtesy of Fisher-Price Toys. ® The Pillsbury Company. Used with permission.

EXHIBIT **23-9.** Television Storyboard Checklist and Evaluation

	Very Good	Good	Fair	Weak	Very Weak
RATIONALE:					
1. Prospect analysis	[ ]	[ ]	[ ]	[ ]	[ ]
2. Advertisement analysis	[ ]	[ ]	[ ]	[ ]	[ ]
CONTENT:					
1. Product identification	[ ]	[ ]	[ ]	[ ]	[ ]
2. Attention-arresting device, opening	[ ]	[ ]	[ ]	[ ]	[ ]
3. Technique, approach appropriate	[ ]	[ ]	[ ]	[ ]	[ ]
4. Simple, clear	[ ]	[ ]	[ ]	[ ]	[ ]
5. Reads smoothly	[ ]	[ ]	[ ]	[ ]	[ ]
6. Focuses on single big idea	[ ]	[ ]	[ ]	[ ]	[ ]
7. Creative, fresh, clever	[ ]	[ ]	[ ]	[ ]	[ ]
8. Audio and video coordinated	[ ]	[ ]	[ ]	[ ]	[ ]
9. Major points repeated	[ ]	[ ]	[ ]	[ ]	[ ]
10. Use of television medium	[ ]	[ ]	[ ]	[ ]	[ ]
11. Strong close	[ ]	[ ]	[ ]	[ ]	[ ]
MISCELLANEOUS:					
1. Mechanics					
A. Times out OK?	[ ]	[ ]	[ ]	[ ]	[ ]
B. Form correct?	[ ]	[ ]	[ ]	[ ]	[ ]
C. Sketches, including color	[ ]	[ ]	[ ]	[ ]	[ ]
2. Overall idea and ad	[ ]	[ ]	[ ]	[ ]	[ ]
3. Spelling and grammar	[ ]	[ ]	[ ]	[ ]	[ ]
4. Followed directions (on time, etc.)	[ ]	[ ]	[ ]	[ ]	[ ]

COMMENTS:

ASSIGNMENT 23-1. Writing a National TV Commercial

Create a 60-second TV spot aimed at the market described below. Do a 30-second spinoff of the 60-second spot.

V-8 Cocktail Vegetable Juice is a canned red juice marketed by the Campbell Soup Company. The product is a blend of eight different natural vegetable juices: tomato, carrot, celery, parsley, beets, spinach, watercress, and lettuce. The blend is approximately 70 percent tomato juice with a 30 percent blend of the other vegetable juices.

Presently, V-8 is packed in four can sizes: 6, 12, 24, and 46 ounces. In addition, a 6-ounce "sleeve pack" (six units per pack) has been marketed with some degree of success. V-8 is distributed primarily in retail grocery and food stores. Some are availble in vending machines. It is priced slightly higher than tomato juice.

According to a survey report, one out of five people sampled used V-8 on a regular basis. The product is used as a breakfast drink; for lunch, dinner, and snacks; as a cocktail ingredient; and in soups. V-8 is currently positioned in the red juice/vegetable juice market. This market is about three-fourths tomato juice and one-fourth vegetable juice.

The principal users and nonusers of V-8, according to research findings, are as follows:

1. A disproportionate amount of vegetable juice is consumed by the 50+ age group. These users account for 57 percent of consumption.
2. Use of V-8 is very low among the younger age groups, especially the 18–24 segment.

It appears that there is a great potential for sales of the product to college students.

ASSIGNMENT 23-2. Writing a Regional TV Commercial

Write a 60-second spot based on the facts given below. The script will be sent to local TV stations in the state of Iowa, to be delivered as an on-camera commercial by the station announcer.

The product is Viravac, an herbicide for soybeans, cotton, sunflowers, and over 50 other crops. Viravac is sold to distributors, who in turn sell to ag-chemical dealers who sell to farmers.

Viravac is an insoluble herbicide that is mixed into the top 2 to 3 inches of soil, where 90 percent of the weed seeds germinate. The farmer may use his own disc or field cultivator to apply the herbicide. Viravac does not need rain to make it work. It stays put because it attaches itself to the surface of the soil particles and organic matter. This is a great advantage over other herbicides, which are less absorptive.

Other advantages: Viravac goes to work immediately to kill susceptible germinating grass, and it keeps working even if there is a heavy rain. It gives long-lasting weed control all summer long, the result of which is a cleaner field with a faster, easier harvest. Additionally, it requires less than other herbicides per acre, affording greater economy and a good return on the farmer's investment.

ASSIGNMENT 23-3. Writing a Local TV Commercial

Write a 60-second spot for a local TV station, based on the facts given below. Do a 30-second spinoff.

The Gateway, a well-established and respected department store, is running a special back-to-school promotion, aimed at college and high school students.

The sale features a nationally known typewriter, which will be sale-priced at $255.75. It is a portable electric, with a cartridge ribbon system for quick, easy change. Black, colored (red, blue, green, brown), and correcting ribbons are available.

The typewriter comes in Aegean Blue, Coppertone, and Norwegian Grey with white accent. It has keyboard controls, repeating action, and either pica or elite type. A durable case is included.

Six extra cartridges will be given away with every typewriter purchased within one week of the announcement.

PART VI
Conclusion

Cases

The authors have found that the use of real products and services for class projects is more meaningful and interesting to students and teachers than the use of hypothetical ones. Students can examine the actual product. They can visit a local store and talk to sales people. And often they can see how the product or service was actually advertised.

There are six advertising/marketing cases presented here for use in advertising copy and layout projects. In each case, the student is provided with background information, a description of the product or service, graphics, and a problem statement for consideration.

In every case, enough information is given to complete several kinds of assignments. However, instructors might find it useful to acquire additional materials from local retailers and manufacturers (brochures, actual ads, etc.) and to bring to class the actual products, if possible. Students are urged to visit local stores to inspect (and even purchase and use) the products or services.

Most of the cases can be used for either retail or national problems. In addition, most of the cases are appropriate for all media and for all kinds of copy and layout assignments (complete ads, headlines only, publicity releases, layouts only, etc.). Even though a suggested problem is given for each case, additional problems relating to specific media and to specific locations may be added.

Honda Passport

History

The first commercial vehicles that could be called the ancestors of motorcycles were built in 1884 by a Philadelphian named Copeland. But the first true motorcycle wasn't made until 1886 in Germany. Other related vehicles developed in the following years in England and France.

The Harley-Davidson Company, the only American survivor today, produced its first motorcycle in 1903, followed by a competitor using the Indian trademark. But the development of the automobile overshadowed and slowed the growth of motorbikes in the United States. However, growth did continue in Britain, Germany, and France.

In the post-World War II period, the French market was dominated by the simple bicycle with a motor. The Italians came into the market with their famous scooters. But, for the most part, the motorcycle industry remained conservative, with models largely unchanged from those in the 1930s.

Background

In 1906, Soichiro Honda was born in Tenuyu City, Japan, the first son of a poor blacksmith and bicycle repairman. Honda seemed to have a natural instinct for machinery and engines, neglecting his studies to tinker with them. In 1922, after only ten years of schooling, he took a job with an automobile repair shop in Tokyo. He gained valuable experience as an apprentice for the next several years.

In 1982, he established a branch of the repair shop with his own capital. He started his own company to produce piston rings and expanded it to manufacture other parts and machinery (including some for the Japanese navy during World War II). He sold the company after the war and invested the profits in a textile company, which had to be closed because of financial problems.

In 1946, Honda established the Honda Technical Research Laboratory to equip bicycles with small army surplus engines. The rest is history. He created the Honda Motor Company in 1948 and produced his model Dream E motorcycle the following year.

EXHIBIT **C-1.** Honda Passport

GET AROUND THE HIGH COST OF GETTING AROUND.

The Honda Passport™ is perfect for all those trips that are too big for the feet, yet too small for the car. You can take it to the theatre. To the park. Or on errands. And you can hardly beat its price or its mileage. It gets up to 130 miles to the gallon.* So not only can you go a long way on it, so can your budget.

The Passport is as easy to ride as it is to park. It has an electric starter for quick starts. And a three-speed transmission with an automatic clutch, so shifting is easy. The Passport will carry one or two comfortably.** And thanks to a 72 cc four-stroke Honda engine, it'll go any city speed limit. You can even carry a little bit extra in the standard front basket and on the rear rack.†

So when four wheels are too many, we've got an economical solution. Get a Honda Passport. It'll fit your life as easily as it fits your budget.

See one at your nearest Honda dealer. There are over 1700 throughout the U.S.

FEATURES:
- Peppy 72 cc OHC, four-stroke engine sips gas but gobbles up miles.
- Electric starter is standard equipment.
- Three-speed transmission with automatic clutch.
- Comfortable seat is under 30 inches high and flips up for refueling.
- Fully enclosed drive chain for less maintenance and extended life.
- Standard front basket and rear carrying rack.

1983 SPECIFICATIONS: PASSPORT (C70)

ENGINE	72 cc. OHC, single-cylinder, four-stroke	BRAKES	Drum
CARBURETOR	14 mm piston valve	TIRES Front:	2.25-17
		Rear:	2.50-17
IGNITION	Flywheel magneto	SUSPENSION Front:	Leading link
		Rear:	Hydraulic shocks
TRANSMISSION	Three-speed	DRY WEIGHT	180.8 pounds
DRIVELINE	Fully enclosed chain	COLORS	Metallic Blue, Metallic Silver
SEAT HEIGHT	29.9 inches		
FUEL CAPACITY	1.1 gallon, including 0.2 gallon reserve	OPTIONAL HONDALINE® EQUIPMENT	Rear baskets

ALWAYS WEAR A HELMET AND EYE PROTECTION. Specifications and availability subject to change without notice.
©1982 American Honda Motor Co., Inc. Printed in U.S.A. AO424
*Estimated mileage calculated from results of emission tests for city riding. You may get different mileage depending on how fast you ride, weather conditions, vehicle load and trip length.
**Maximum load capacity 300 pounds.
†Do not exceed basket or rack load limits.

HONDA
FOLLOW THE LEADER

The company produced a sports car in 1963 and a lightweight passenger car in 1967. Honda retired as president in 1973, becoming his firm's "supreme adviser."

Advertising

Realizing the vast potential for sales of two-wheel vehicles in the United States, Honda formed American Honda in Los Angeles in June 1959. The new company broke tradition with motorbike advertising from the very beginning. Instead of using typical motorbike media, ads were aimed at the masses in magazines such as *Time, Look,* and *Life*—unprecedented at that time. Later, all major media were added. In 1964, the company ran commercials on the widely-watched Academy Awards telecast, spreading the Honda name nationwide.

From the start, Honda appealed to the general public. First, the company used as its slogan "You meet the nicest people on a Honda." Later, it used "The nicest things happen on a Honda." American Honda currently spends over $21 million annually on advertising in virtually all media, with such slogans as "Follow the leader, he's on a Honda" and "Honda, we make it simple."

The Product

In June 1958, Honda produced the first step-through motorbike. This unique design not only revolutionized the Honda company, but also established an industry in Japan that has dominated the entire world's business in the motorbike field. Competitors include Suzuki, Yamaha, and Kawasaki.

Among the most popular models is the Honda Passport. Its features include the following:

- 72cc, four-stroke, single-cylinder engine
- Electric starter
- Three-speed transmission with automatic clutch
- Comfortable seat under 30 inches high
- Fully enclosed drive chain
- Standard front basket and rear carrying rack
- Up to 130 miles per gallon

The Problem

All motorbikes still suffer from negative images. They are identified with gangs, racing, accidents, etc. With the high costs of automobiles and gasoline, however, more and more people are looking for alternative modes of transportation. Two-wheel vehicles such as the Passport have an opportunity to fill that need.

Orville Redenbacher's Gourmet Popping Corn

Background

Orville Redenbacher's Gourmet Popping Corn is a special hybrid popping corn. After many years of selective breeding, Orville Redenbacher developed a popping corn that was better tasting, popped bigger kernels,

EXHIBIT **C-2.** Orville Redenbacher's Gourmet Popping Corn

HOW TO POP MY SUPERIOR POPPING CORN PERFECTLY MOST EVERY TIME

Use the Right Utensil — You can use almost any utensil. An electric popper or any pot or skillet – as long as the bottom is heavy and the lid **allows the steam to escape.** If it can't, the popped corn will turn out tough and soggy, so leave popper or pan lid slightly ajar.

Use the Right Oil — Use my **GOURMET®** BUTTERY FLAVOR® Popping Oil, for delicious taste without adding butter calories. If you prefer oil without the taste of butter, I recommend WESSON® oil.

Measure Carefully:	Popper Size	My Popcorn	Oil
	4 Quart	1/2 Cup	3 Tablespoons
	3 Quart	1/3 Cup	2 Tablespoons

Follow These Directions:

1. Measure the oil into popper (see above for specific amount), drop in three kernels, cover and heat. Use medium-high heat for skillets or pots.
2. When one kernel pops, carefully add remaining measure of corn and cover. Shake pan or skillet to evenly heat every kernel.
3. When popping slows, unplug cord or remove from heat. Remove from pan when popping stops.
4. Add salt as desired after popping. Adding salt before popping toughens the corn. If you wish, add butter (unless you used my BUTTERY FLAVOR Popping Oil).

Reseal jar after use and store at room temperature. It keeps my popping corn as fresh as can be.

HOT AIR POPPING — As you know, my popcorn pops up bigger and fluffier than other brands because we control the moisture content of each kernel for maximum "popping explosion". This same powerful "popping explosion" that makes my corn so "melt-in-your-mouth" good, may also blow a few of the kernels out of your hot air popper before they get a chance to pop. That's because today's hot air popping machines can't quite handle the extra-strong "popping explosion" of my **GOURMET®** Popping Corn. If your machine lets a few kernels sneak out unpopped, just put them back into the popper and give 'em another chance. They'll pop up big and fluffy, too!

DIST. BY HUNT-WESSON FOODS, INC., FULLERTON, CA 92634   © H.W.F.I.

"MY GOURMET® POPPING CORN IS THE FINEST IN THE WORLD. AND NOW IT'S VACUUM PACKED EXTRA FRESH".

I've loved popping corn as long as I can remember. I've devoted my life to experimenting, cross breeding and hybridizing over 40 generations of corn to create this perfect popping corn, which pops up fluffy and great tasting.

But, my special corn isn't the only secret. Extra care at harvest time is important too. Unlike "ordinary" popcorns, my **GOURMET®** Popping Corn is dried and shelled ear by ear. And after every kernel is sorted and polished, it's then **VACUUM PACKED EXTRA FRESH** in resealable glass jars which preserve moisture for maximum pop.

You can actually see the difference. My **GOURMET®** Popping Corn pops up much more than ordinary popcorns. It's light and fluffy too. And, because it's packed fresh, virtually every kernel pops into a tasty morsel, first batch to last.

You'll taste the difference too. Every mouthful is deliciously light and tender. It's guaranteed fresh or your money back.

Do try my **GOURMET** Brand Popping Corn. You'll like it better, or my name isn't... Orville Redenbacher

Orville Redenbacher

SOURCE: Hunt-Wesson Foods, Inc./Fullerton, CA 92634

and popped more completely than ordinary popcorn. Hunt-Wesson Foods, Inc., discovered Orville's corn in a supermarket in the Midwest. When the company learned that the product was selling quite well at a premium price, it obtained national marketing rights to Orville and his corn.

The Product

In tests by an independent research firm, respondents preferred Orville Redenbacher Popping Corn to all other brands by two to one in terms of taste (best), volume (largest), and unpopped kernels (fewest). They also liked its lightness, tenderness, and fluffiness. It comes in 15-ounce and 30-ounce glass jars. These give the popping corn a top quality appearance, support the premium price structure, and increase in-home life and freshness. For several years, the slogan used by the brand was "The world's most expensive popping corn." Since dropped as a slogan, it still *is* expensive, however, with an average price per pound of $.99, compared to ordinary popping corn, which costs approximately $.39.

The Market

The retail market for packaged popcorn sold through grocery store outlets is estimated to be over $80 million annually. Most popcorn is sold in one-pound and two-pound cellophane bags. The market is very fractionated and regionalized, with over 85 brands competing. Private or store brands represent about 40 percent of the market (share of volume). Leading share brands include Jolly Time, Pops-Rite, 3-Minute, and Jiffy Pop, none of which has over a 15 percent dollar or volume share. No single brand has true national distribution.

In addition to ORPC's unique packaging, three other popping corns boast innovations. Jiffy Pop and Presto Pop come in an aluminum foil package shaped like a skillet, ready to heat on the stove top. TV Time's package includes a pot of coconut oil.

Consumption is somewhat regionally skewed, with heavier usage in the Midwest, the traditional cornbelt. However, growth of consumption has been extremely high in the West and South. The Northeast still has the lowest per capita consumption of popcorn and thus has the greatest potential.

Consumer Profile

Members of the family other than the housewife have a great influence on the purchase and usage of popcorn, much more so than most other grocery products. National syndicated research indicates 56 percent of homemakers use popcorn. By age, the usage categories are 35–49 (36.9 percent), 25–34 (24.6 percent), and 50–64 (18.5 percent).

Media Support

The annual advertising budget for ORPC is approximately $6 million. Advertising media include daytime and nightime network television, spot television, women's magazines, newspapers, and trade publications. Promotion activities include: official popcorn at Disneyland and Disney World, discount coupons in corn poppers, a Flying Kernel Hot-Air Balloon, and a five-minute syndicated television interview and film featuring Orville Redenbacher.

Objectives

The marketing objective is to market a high quality popping corn at a premium price in order to generate new sales and profit dollars. Specific advertising objectives include: (1) creating awareness of the product; (2) justifying the high premium price of the product; and (3) assuring consumer identification of the package.

EXHIBIT **C-3.** Pitney Bowes Postage Meter

The Pitney Bowes Touchmatic Postage Meter
Gives Your Outgoing Mail the Uncommon Touch

You can put the benefits of metered mail at your fingertips with the Pitney Bowes Touchmatic Postage Meter. Because the keyboard is just like the keyboard of a touch-telephone or a calculator. You can print up metered-mail postage amounts in a matter of seconds.

But the benefits of the Touchmatic go far beyond its convenient, color-coded touch keyboard. Because Touchmatic gives you all the convenience, security, efficiency, speed, flexibility, prestige, versatility and productivity of metered mail...even if you're a small volume mailer.

With the PB Touchmatic, you can print envelopes with any denomination of postage—from 1¢ to $9.99—or print postage for packages and over-sized envelopes directly on gummed labels, ready for affixing. And if you like, you can simultaneously print your own meter ad or message.

What's more, the Touchmatic postage meter can hold from $20 to $9,999 worth of postage, saving you trips to the post office. And the high-capacity, disposable inker can make thousands of impressions before being replaced.

Touchmatic is compact...about the same size as a desk phone. Attractive. Fits in with any office decor. And it comes with its own lightweight carrying case.

• Select postage value by pressing appropriate buttons on the *keyboard.* Touch control sharply reduces mistakes in postage setting.

• After positioning the envelope, just touch the *"trip"* key.

• Correct mistakes with the *clear-button.*

• *Registers* automatically show postage used and postage remaining.

• *Dollar-lock button* must be pushed for denominations of $1.00 or more. Prevents accidental overcharge. It also secures the machine to prevent unauthorized use.

• Handy *date-change dial* enables you to change the imprint date in seconds.

• If your mail goes out in a stack at a time—rather than a piece at a time—the optional *Model 5830 Mailing Machine* base will add feeding, sealing and stacking...all in one, automatic operation.

Specifications:

Overall Height: 5½" (140 mm)

Base Dimensions: 11" x 6½" (279 mm x 165 mm)

Weight: 13 lbs. (6 kg)

Finish: Off-white and black enamel casing

The Touchmatic offers you all the benefits of metered mail.

1. Postal consultation and service. You get free, no-obligation counsel from PB mailing professionals on any aspect of mail/paper-handling procedures.

2. Postage convenience. Print the *exact* amount of postage you need—whenever you need it—for any kind or class of mail. Fewer trips to the post office.

3. Automatic postage accounting. Your meter keeps track of postage used and on-hand, automatically. You can see at a glance how much you've used, how much is left.

4. Office efficiency. Imprint postage, seal and postmark your mail. Give employees more time to do more important and productive work.

5. Improved office morale. Make employees happier on the job by eliminating tiresome wetting and sticking of stamps and envelopes.

6. Package and large envelope capability. For a neat and dated, professional-looking package, your meter will produce gummed meter tapes for the exact amount of postage you need.

7. Faster postal service. Because your mail is already dated and canceled, it moves through the post office faster and often catches earlier trucks and planes.

8. Professional image. Your mail looks neat, crisp, modern and business-like...and that carries a message about *you* and your organization.

9. Meter advertising. Use the *free* advertising space on your outgoing envelopes to create low-cost, high-impact advertising campaigns. Ask your PB representative for our free catalog of postage meter ads.

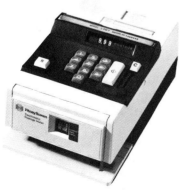

Walter H. Wheeler, Jr., Drive
Stamford, Connecticut 06926

SOURCE: Courtesy of Pitney Bowes.

Pitney Bowes Postage Meter

Background

Pitney Bowes invented the postage meter and received government permission to market the product in 1920. Postage meters are machines leased to business firms, who then take a cartridge from the machine to the post office to pay for postage and have the meter set for some amount. The meter allows firms to mail when the post office is closed, to avoid using stamps, to send professional-looking mailings, and to minimize pilfering. The meter stamping also allows the advertiser to put a brief advertising message on the envelope.

The Problem

Pitney Bowes dominates the postage meter market but still does not have complete saturation. The problem is to find those firms that do not now have postage meter systems and to reach those interested in looking into the possibility of using such a system. Most large businesses use such systems, so the target market tends to be small businesses.

Strategy

The Pitney Bowes company wants to reach smaller businesses in the major metropolitan areas in the country through chamber of commerce magazines, city magazines, and such business publications as *Nation's Business, Business Week,* and *Business World.* The emphasis should be on telling nonusers of postage meter systems why they should use the system, and on getting inquiries for use by the sales department. Although business advertising often uses technical language, in this case the emphasis should be more on conversational, personal case history copy.

The specific model to emphasize is the Touchmatic 5707, the smallest and least expensive of the company's postage meters. It is slightly larger than a desk telephone. It prints postage, a dated postmark, and an optional ad and seals envelopes.

Holiday Inn Hotels

Background

In 1952, one year after a young man from Tennessee took a trip with his family and tried to find a decent place to stay, he opened the first Holiday Inn in his hometown of Memphis. That young man, Kemmons Wilson, went on to make Holiday Inns the largest hotel chain in the world before retiring in 1979. Today, the Holiday Inn hotel system is comprised of more than 1,760 hotels and 312,000 rooms in 57 countries. In 1982, the hotels served approximately 120 million people and produced an estimated $4 billion in revenues.

Today, the Holiday Inn hotel system continues to grow, with a massive building program underway that will see the chain add a new property almost every seven days through 1984. Emphasis continued to be placed on improving system-wide product quality. The Holiday Inn hotel system includes both franchised hotels, which are licensed by Memphis-based Holiday Inns, Inc., and company-owned and operated properties.

EXHIBIT **C-4.**   Holiday Inn Motels

APPROVED GRAPHICS—DOMESTIC
Holiday Inns, Inc.—Corporate Identity
3742 Lamar Ave., Memphis, Tennessee 38118 U.S.A. 901/362-4484

SOURCE: Courtesy of Holiday Inns, Inc.

The Product

Since its beginning over 30 years ago, Holiday Inns, Inc., has set the standard for facilities and features in the hospitality industry. The very first Holiday Inn offered guest rooms with private baths, air conditioning, and telephones. Other features included swimming pools, free ice, free parking, and dog kennels. Children under 12 could stay free. These amenities—which are common today—were revolutionary for the hotel industry at that time.

Holiday Inns, Inc., has continued to introduce innovations throughout its hotel system. These include computerized reservations (the Holidex II utilizes state-of-the-art technology), the HI-NET video-conferencing network via satellite, HBO in-room movies at no extra charge, Holidome indoor recreation centers, and money-back "No Excuses"® Room Guarantee program.

The company recently announced a program of extensive refurbishment of existing rooms and properties. By the end of 1983, more than 60 percent of Holiday Inn hotels worldwide had been extensively remodeled or built within the previous five years.

Holiday Inns, Inc., has introduced a new worldwide chain of upscale, high-rise hotels that offer superior services, amenities, and standards. The new brand is identified as Holiday Inn Crowne Plaza hotels and is being developed, marketed, and operated under the Holiday Inn hotel umbrella.

Advertising

Holiday Inns, Inc., has been an active advertiser throughout its history. Some of its memorable advertising slogans and campaigns from over the years include "The Best Surprise Is No Surprise," "Welcome to Some of the Best Hotels in the World," and "Number 1 in People Pleasin'."

In mid-1983, the company introduced a new national advertising campaign telling consumers why Holiday Inns are "A Better Place to Be." The campaign spotlights new hotels and major innovations and is designed to show that Holiday Inn is a contemporary, growing hotel chain that continues to lead the lodging industry in the 1980s.

As with all national advertisers, Holiday Inns, Inc., uses most major media, including network and spot television and radio, magazines, newspapers, and outdoor. In addition, individual Holiday Inn hotels take advantage of the local media in their areas to communicate with local and transient customers.

The Problem

Holiday Inns, Inc., will continue to be the leader in the hotel industry. The sheer numbers of locations and rooms—and the plans to increase both—will solidify its dominance in the travel-lodging field.

In an area in which the company sees good potential for growth is that of serving the communities in which Inns are located. Such services include food and entertainment for local people and meeting facilities for businesses and organizations. These people need to be told of these opportunities.

Virtually all Holiday Inns include restaurants. Many have bars and clubs and offer live entertainment. Most properties have meeting facilities, ranging from modest meeting rooms in smaller Inns to large convention complexes in larger Inns. Holidomes feature climate-controlled swimming pools, miniature golf, exercise rooms, saunas, sidewalk cafes, electronic game areas, ping pong, and shuffleboard, all in spacious, landscaped enclosures.

Texas Fireframe Grate

Background

In September 1975, a new way of making fire in the fireplace was introduced. It was discovered by Dr. Lawrence Cranberg, a consulting physicist in Austin, Texas, after he saw the need for fundamental improvements in the ancient art of fire-making. Analyzing the conventional three-log fire, Cranberg discovered that heat is trapped in the middle of the logs. He found that heat could be released by lifting and supporting the top log and thereby creating a "slot." This principle of "slot geometry," or "slot flame stability," as Cranberg named it, let to the design of a fireplace grate that would capitalize on the concept. By experimenting with several size logs and positions, Cranberg concluded that a large log in the back, a medium-sized log on top, and two small logs in front give maximum performance. This performance includes the following:

EXHIBIT **C-5.**   Texas Fireframe Grate

TEXAS FIREFRAME Co.

P.O. Box 3435   Austin, Texas 78764

Phone 512-327-1794

TEXAS FIREFRAME® GRATE

Turns your fireplace into a real heating unit.

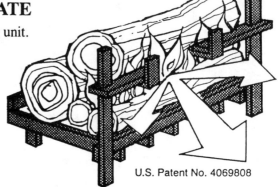

U.S. Patent No. 4069808

- Throws much more heat into room.
- Starts Easily with unsplit logs.
- No log–turning to keep the fire going.
- It saves fuel.
- Sizes for every fireplace and Franklin Stove.
- Feel warmth 10–12 feet from fire.
- Control the rate of burning with height-adjustable arms.
- Reduces risk of chimney fires.
- Engineered for convenience and durability.
- Simple, copyrighted instructions.

"It channels an amazing amount of heat from a fireplace directly into the room, without any moving parts."   *Better Homes and Gardens*

"Easy lighting is a side benefit of this grate arrangement; the big advantage is the slow-burning steady fire that results . . ."   *The New York Times*

"Forces a fire not only to burn better but to send more of its heat into the room."   *Time Magazine*

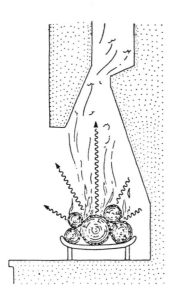

Conventional grate radiation pattern.

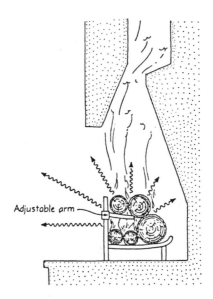

Adjustable arm

Texas Fireframe grate radiation pattern.

SOURCE: Courtesy of Texas Fireframe Co.

1. A great reduction or elimination of the risk of chimney fires since the fire is capped from above, resulting in a truly safe way to make a log fire.
2. A steady, even burning of the logs, particularly the front two.
3. An easy-to-start fire, with only a match and very little paper.
4. Elimination of constant tending and the need to stir and poke.
5. More efficient heating because heat is directed outward, not upward.
6. New front logs are ignited without rekindling by radiation.

The Product

The Texas Fireframe is an all-welded, heavy-duty grate, made from hot-rolled steel bars. It looks much like conventional grates, but the front legs are much taller and have adjustable arms on which the top log rests. The fire-making method and the grate are protected by U.S. Patent No. 4069808, and the instructions are copyrighted. There are two sizes:

1. Model KS-25. 25″ front, 21″ back, 15″ high, 13″ deep. 30 lb. $54.95, shipping included. Black.
2. Model U17. 17″ front, 14″ back, 13″ high, 13″ deep. 21 lb. $39.95, shipping included. Black.

The Market

Primary sale of the product to date has been through mail order from the company. Limited distribution has been through dealers, mainly hardware stores. Units have been sold and dealers are located throughout the country, with no emphasis on a particular region. Buying of the product is seasonal, with the following patterns to date: January–March, 11 percent; April–June, 1 percent; July–September, 22 percent; and October–December, 66 percent.

A special Target Group Index (TGI) tabulation indicates that one in five households or apartments nationally has a fireplace. The percentage is somewhat higher (one in three) for the western states.

Promotion

Texas Fireframe has been advertised nationally in such media as the *Wall Street Journal, Scientific American, Organic Gardening,* and *Country Gentleman.* It also has been advertised regionally in *Texas Monthly, Sunset,* and the Pacific Northwest edition of *Time.* The revolutionary nature of the prduct has resulted in phenomenal publicity, including an article in *Time* on December 22, 1975, which gave the new fire-making method the name "Physicist's Fire," a feature on CBS Morning news, and an article in *American Home,* among many others.

The Problem

Dr. Cranberg would like to reduce the percentage of sales by mail order and increase distribution by dealers to a 50-50 split. He wants a dual aggressive advertising approach, aimed at (1) prime prospects, to convince them to purchase a grate (either directly by mail order or locally); and (2) potential dealers (hardware stores), to convince them to stock and promote the product.

Sidles Auto Sun Shades

Background

In 1953, R. H. Sidles developed the first application of louvered screen for sun control in automobiles. After further research and experimentation, he applied for patents on his invention and formed a company to manufacture and market the product. Sidles Manufacturing Company was formed during 1954 in Laredo, Texas. A need for a more central plant led to the move of the firm's manufacturing facilities to Temple, Texas, in 1955. Temple is in the exact center of the state.

The Product

Sidles Custom Auto Sun Shades are fabricated from Kaiser Shade-Screen, a louvered, aluminum sun-deflecting screen. This screen material blocks the direct rays of the sun from the interior of a vehicle, thereby increasing the efficiency of air conditioning operation, reducing glare, and adding privacy to the interior of a vehicle. The product is a sun control device. Some of the firm's screens—those at an angle on rear windows—are made from Phifer Sun Screen, also aluminum.

The screens are custom made. That is, every window for every model and brand of car has its own screen. This offers both maximum efficiency and attractive appearance.

Each screen has aluminum edging and ribs to keep it rigid. When placed in a vertical position, this screening material (which is composed of thousands of small louvers permanently tilted downwards at a 17-degree angle) blocks up to 78 percent of the direct radiation of the sun. Although it may appear that the shades are interchangeable from side to side, they are not. There is a definite inside and outside to the Kaiser ShadeScreen. One side keeps out the sun; the other lets you see through.

The Promotion

The original Sidles Auto Sun Shades were standardized, not custom made. This allowed them to be distributed through any auto parts store or other appropriate retail firm. But as increased emphasis was placed on the customizing feature, inventory became a problem for dealers. In addition, further emphasis was placed on mail order sales as a complete inventory of patterns was accumulated. Now, virtually all sales are through mail order.

The company uses consumer magazines exclusively for advertising and promotion. Current magazines used by the company include *Sunset, Southern Living, Trailer Life, Motor Trend, AKC Gazette,* and *Elks Magazine.* In addition, editorial features are given to the company from time to time in the shopper sections.

Scott Sidles, company president, recently has added a toll-free telephone number for Texas (1-800-792-3030) and for outside Texas (1-800-433-3101). Also, he has been experimenting with showing a variety of vehicles in his ads (vans, station wagons, hatchbacks, etc.) and has found an increased response from owners of each of these as advertised.

EXHIBIT **C-6.** *Sidles Auto Sun Shades*

ORDER BLANK Date_____

Ship to: Name_____

Address_____Phone_____

City_____State_____Zip_____

Make_____**Series**_____

Year_____Model: **2-Door** ☐ **4-Door** ☐

Wagon ☐   **Sedan** ☐   **Hard Top** ☐

Part Number   Price per Pair

Front doors _____   _____

Rear doors _____   _____

Rear quarter_____   _____

Rear view _____   _____

Other   _____   _____

% Sales Tax (Texas orders only)_____
**10% POSTAGE & HANDLING must
be included** on orders for less than
three part numbers   _____

Total . . . .   ══════════

☐ Charge to my Master Charge

Card #_____

4 digit number over my name   _____

"Good Thru" date
and letter code_____

SIDLES MANUFACTURING CO., INC.
Box 3537 — Temple, Texas 76501

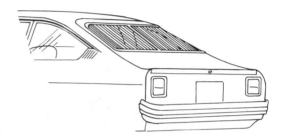

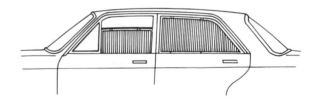

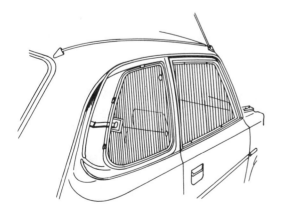

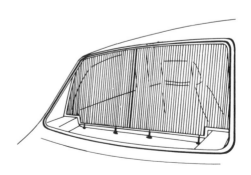

SOURCE: Used by permission, R. Scott Sidles.

The Problem

The problem is to "sell" Sidles Auto Sun Shades entirely in a mail order advertisement. This means, of course, that you will include all necessary information anticipated to be important to the prospect in making an inquiry into the product. Usually the prospect will send the make, model, and year of the car or other vehicle being considered for the screens. Only then will specific prices be quoted and other ordering information given. Consumer magazines, then, are used to make the initial contact, with direct mail used for the follow-up.

Glossary

Above the line. Costs relating to creative elements in production, which usually include such areas as acting, directing, script writing, and music.

Account. An advertiser. Also called *client.*

Account executive. A person in an ad agency in charge of advertising for an account. May be called *account supervisor.*

Ad. An abbreviation for advertisement.

Adjacencies. Commercials placed next to certain programing: news, weather, sports.

Affidavit. A sworn statement by a station that commercials were on air in certain time periods.

Affiliate. An independently owned station that provides some of its time for network programs and advertising. The remainder of the broadcast day is programmed locally.

Agate line. A line of type set in 5½ point type. Also, a unit of measurement for ad space, one column wide and 1/14 inch deep.

Agency commission. The percentage (usually 15 percent) of billing allowed to an accredited advertising agency when it places time or space for an advertiser.

Aided recall. One method of radio audience survey in which the interviewer provides respondents with a frame of reference to assist their memory about listening.

Airbrush. A commercial art method of retouching by spraying paint on a photograph or artwork.

Air-check. A tape made of a commercial or program at the time of airing.

Album rock format. Young-adult targeted, plays selections from popular rock albums usually in uninterrupted segments.

AM. Technically, amplitude modulation: practically, 540 to 1600 kilohertz on the radio dial.

Angled. A poster panel position in which one end of the panel is six feet or more farther back from the road than the other end.

Announcement. A commercial or spot. A radio commercial message of 60, 30, or 10 seconds.

Approach. The distance from the point where an outdoor unit becomes visible to the point where it ceases to be visible.

Apron. The lattice or other decorative finish immediately below the bottom of an outdoor unit.

Arbitron (formerly ARB). A radio ratings organization that uses a diary method to survey audience listenership primarily by sex and age. Also conducts phone surveys in some markets.

Art director. The advertising agency specialist who is responsible for visual effects.

ASCAP. American Society of Composers, Authors and Publishers.

Audience survey. A study of the radio audience in a given market. Usually shows the percentage of people listening to radio; the percentage of total listeners for each station (share of audience); the total number of people tuned to each station (cumes). Arbitron uses the diary method, Pulse an interview technique, but both survey individuals.

Audio. Refers to the sound portion of a TV commercial.

Availabilities. Time slots in which commercials can be placed. To call for "avails" is to contact the station salesmen to see what time slots are open.

Background. Often abbreviated to BG and referring to the setting behind the actors or products in the foreground.

Bait advertising. Also called *bait and switch*. Advertising that lures people into stores for bargains, then switches to a higher-priced product. The advertised product is often difficult or impossible to buy.

Baseboard. A white paper border surrounding the poster copy area.

Beautiful music format. Uninterrupted segments of melodic music arrangements. Little talk or news; frequently automated.

Below the line. Costs relating to noncreative elements in production: the technical or materials areas. These may include sets, equipment, and props.

Ben day. A process of mechanically adding tone or pattern to a line reproduction.

Billboard. The announcement that gives sponsor and/or product identification at the beginning of a TV broadcast.

Black format. Frequently features community and black news as well as music chosen for the black community.

Blank out. The covering of all, or a portion, of a poster design.

Bleed-face bulletin. Painting of the copy to the extreme edge, eliminating the molding.

Bleed posting. A poster arrangement in which the paper goes to the molding without blanking at top or sides.

Blocking. Roughing out camera and cast positions and movement before actual filming begins.

Blowup. An enlargement.

Body copy. Text material set in blocks in relatively small type. Distinguished from display copy (headlines and subheadlines and other larger type).

Body type. Type set 12 points and smaller, used for body copy. Distinguished from display type, 14 points and larger.

Boldface (bf). Heavy, black type.

Border. Rule (line) or design art that surrounds an ad and defines its edges. All ads do not have to have borders.

Box. A design element, enclosing part of an ad with rules.

Brainstorming. A group meeting in which spontaneous ideas are randomly presented as a means of solving problems or developing plans.

Brand name. The name given to a specific product, i.e., Chevrolet. (See *trade name*.)

Broadcasting. As a noun, either of the electronic media: radio or television. As a verb, sending out a signal on the airwaves that's capable of being received by radio or television sets.

BTA. Same as *run of schedule*: station schedules BTA or ROS announcements at the best time slots available. If better times become available, spots will be upgraded.

Bulk discount. An earned discount for quantity purchases: the larger the quantity, the greater the discount per unit.

Bulk plan. A popular retail contract in which a retailer commits to buy a certain number of radio spots in one year. Also called contract year.

Busy. A condition in design in which there are too many elements for the space, and they compete with each other for attention. Also referred to as *cluttered*.

Call letters. The station's name assigned by the Federal Communications Commission: e.g., WWWW. Most stations east of the Mississippi River have call letters beginning with "W"; west of the Mississippi, call letters generally begin with "K."

Camera-ready. A paste-up or slick ready to be photographed. No type is to be set; no further treatment is needed.

Campaign. Planned advertising on radio or in other media.

Caps. In typography, capital (or uppercase) letters.

Caps and lowercase (clc). Capital and small letters. Use initial caps where appropriate.

Caption. The text accompanying a photograph or illustration.

Cart. A cartridge case containing ¼" magnetic tape used by stations instead of separate reels of commercials or programs. Carts are easy to handle, semiautomatic.

Cassette. ⅛" magnetic tape cartridge convenient for listening to sound and recording actualities due to its ease of play-back.

Center spread. An advertisement covering the two facing pages in the center of a publication, on a single sheet of paper. Also called *double-truck*.

Character. Any individual letter, number, punctuation mark, or space in printed matter. A unit of type.

Chase. A steel frame in which type is locked up for press.

Checking copy. A copy of a publication sent to an advertiser for proofing or to prove that the ad was actually run as ordered.

Circulation. The number of copies of a publication distributed or sold. It can be measured accurately and is often audited. To be distinguished from *readership*. *In broadcast media, a term used to describe the side of the cumulative audience of a station or a network over some specific period of time.*

Circulation (daily effective). Individuals who have a reasonable opportunity of observing an outdoor display—usually half of all people passing in cars and trucks and 25 percent of all mass-transit passengers.

City zone. That portion of a newspaper's coverage area that includes the corporate city and adjacent areas that have the characteristics of the city.

Classical format. Radio format featuring classical music.

Classified advertising. Small-type, usually brief all-copy ads grouped according to product or service. Most are from individuals, but businesses use them also. See *display classified*.

Cliche. A word or phrase used too often to be effective in either headlines or copy.

Client. An advertiser. See *account*.

Clip book. A book, often looseleaf, with pages of stock art (usually on slick paper), ready for paste-up or photographing.

Close-up. A shot of an individual or an object (usually the product) with the camera moved in close. If the shot is of a person, it will show only the head and shoulders.

Closed circuit. Nonbroadcast transmission of a television image to a receiver, not the general public.

Closing date. The deadline for submitting an ad to a medium.

Cold type. Type composed by photographic means, paper pasteup, or typewriter.

Collating posters. Arranging poster sheets into the order in which they will be posted.

Color separation. Process of breaking down full-color art into its primary color components.

Column inch. A unit of space, one column wide by one inch deep.

Combination plate. An engraving that combines line and halftone reproduction.

Combination rate. A special rate for advertising in two or more publications under the same ownership (often morning and evening editions) or two or more radio stations, such as "sister" AM and FM stations or two stations with geographical tie-in.

Commercial. An announcement or spot. A radio sales message.

Commission system. A method of payment to an advertising agency; the agency gets 15% of what the client spends for space. The agency bills the client the cost of the ad, then pays the medium 85 percent of the total.

Composite print. A film print containing both picture and sound track.

Comprehensive (comp). A layout prepared to resemble the finished ad as closely as possible.

Condensed type. Type with characters narrower than the regular face, permitting more characters per inch. (Opposite of extended type.)

Continuity. Radio copy, scripts for commercials.

Control room. The room in which video and/ or audio are coordinated.

Controlled circulation. The circulation of a publication (usually business) sent free to individuals selected by job category. Many are still audited.

Cooperative (co-op) advertising. Usually refers to advertising paid for jointly by a manufacturer and a retailer. Often called vendor advertising. The term is also applied to advertising sponsored by several normally competing firms. The former is vertical; the latter, horizontal.

Copy. Usually, the written material or text matter of an ad. Sometimes, however, the word is used to refer to all elements in the finished ad, including art.

Copy fitting. Estimating how much space copy will take when it is set in type, by character count or word count methods.

Copy platform. The statement of the basic ideas to be used in an ad or campaign and their relative importance. Listing of selling points and benefits and instructions regarding policy in handling elements in the ad(s). Also called copy policy, copy outline, copy plan.

Copy sheet. An 8½″ × 11″ sheet of typing paper on which all text material to be in the ad is typed and keyed to the layout.

Corporate advertising. Advertising that emphasizes the company behind a product or service rather than the product or service itself. Also called *institutional advertising*.

Cost per thousand (CPM). How much it costs to reach 1,000 prospects with an ad. May be CPM readers, viewers, or listeners. If a station delivers 30,000 listeners for a $45 spot, the CPM is $1.50.

Country format. A radio format playing modern country music. "Nashville sound."

Coverage area. The geographical area potentially reached by a station.

Crop. To eliminate unwanted areas in a piece of art or photograph or to change its proportions to desired ones.

Cumulative audience. Also called *cume*. The audience reached by a station over an extended period, such as a daypart or combination of dayparts or a full week.

Cut. Trade term for art in plate form, ready to print, for letterpress printing.

Cut outs. The letters, packages, figures, or mechanical devices attached to the face of a painted bulletin to provide a three-dimensional effect.

Cut to. A quick change of scene; going from the picture on one camera to the picture on another almost instantaneously.

Day-glo. The trade name of inks and lacquers that fluoresce in sunlight or backlight.

Daytime. A radio time slot, usually 10 A.M. to 3 P.M.

Deadline. The day or hour after which advertising will not be accepted for appearance in a specific edition of a publication. See *closing date*.

Demographics. The statistical description of prospects in physical terms, such as age, sex, occupation, marital status, education, household income, etc.

Dial position. Where station is found on radio dial.

Diary. A method of surveying the radio audience in which the diary-keeper fills in times he or she listened to the radio.

Direct advertising. Printed advertising other than that which appears in publications. Delivered by mail, salesmen, dealers, etc. Does not include posters or point-of-purchase advertising.

Disc jockey or deejay. An on-air personality. Besides playing records, he may provide service information, make entertaining comments, and give commercials.

Disco format. A radio format featuring up-tempo, rock dance music.

Display ad. An ad in a newspaper using art or graphic elements (such as illustrations, varying type, white space, or color) in contrast to all-copy classified ads.

Display classified. Classified ads that include art, display type, and other elements of display ads. They are usually used by businesses rather than individuals.

Display type. Type larger than 12 point, used for headlines and other emphasized elements.

Dissolve. Fading in a new scene while fading out an old one, usually used to connote a lapse of time.

Dolly. The camera is mounted on wheels so that it can dolly in for a close-up or dolly out for a longer shot.

Double decker. One panel built directly above another.

Double truck. Also, *double-page spread,* or *center spread.* The two facing pages on a single sheet in the center of a publication or individual section.

Down-and-under. A direction in the script that calls for sound effects, music, or voice to be heard at a lower level.

Downstyle. A style characterized by the use of lowercase letters in headlines except for the first letters of first words of sentences and for the first letters of proper names. It is considered more modern than capitalizing every word in headlines.

Drive time. The morning and afternoon hours when many listeners drive to and from work or shopping. Also called AM Drive (usually 5 to 10 A.M.) and PM Drive (usually 3 to 7 P.M.). Drive time can also be referred to as traffic, commuter, or triple A time.

Dummy. A mockup of the finished product, showing where the elements will be placed.

Duplicate plates. Copies of original plates for distribution to several publications.

Earned rate. The rate an advertiser pays for space (or time) actually used within a specific period of time.

ECU. Stands for extreme close-up; a shot with the camera in so close that only a portion of a face or object is seen.

Editorial matter. Anything appearing in a publication that is not advertising (including news and entertainment).

Electrotype. A duplicate plate.

Element. Any one of the distinguishable components of an ad: headline, subheadline, body copy, illustration, logo, border, etc.

Em. The square of any type size, thus the spacing equal to it. Unless otherwise specified, the pica-em, or 1/6 inch.

Embellishments. The extensions attached to painted or printed bulletins. Standard OAAA embellishment sizes are 5'6" at the top, 2' at sides, and 1' to 2' at bottom.

End rate. The lowest rate at which a station offers commercial time.

Engraving. Also *photoengraving*. An original printing plate.

Evening. A radio time slot, usually from 7 P.M. to midnight.

Expanded type. Also extended type. The opposite of condensed type. Characters are wider than normal or regular.

Face. The style or design of type.

Facing. Specifies the direction of the poster face relative to traffic flow. A south-facing panel can be read by northbound traffic.

Fact sheet. An outline of a product's selling points and other facts given to copywriters.

Fade-in. The transition from a black screen to an image.

Fade-out. The opposite of the above; the picture gradually disappears until the screen is dark.

Fair trade. Laws that restrain retailers from selling products at prices lower than those established by agreement between manufacturer and retailer.

Family. In typography, one design of type in a complete range of sizes and variations.

Feedback. In communication, the response or reaction by the receiver of a message, indicating how it is being interpreted.

File proof. Proof of an ad for record purposes.

Flag. A tear in a poster causing paper to hang loose.

Flatbed. A letterpress printing press that prints from flat bed, rather than round or rotary cylinder. Slower than rotary.

Flat rate. A uniform rate for ad space, with no discounts for volume or frequency.

Flush. Printed matter set even or aligned at left (flush left), right (flush right), or both (flush left and right, also called justified).

Font. A complete set of type characters of a particular typeface and size.

Formal balance. In design, the symmetrical arrangement of elements.

Foundry type. Hand-set metal type.

Four-color process. A printing process that reproduces a full range of colors using red, yellow, blue and black. *Full color.*

Frame. Refers to the individual picture element. Twenty-four frames are exposed each second by the cameras at normal sound speed.

Freeze frame. Holding a specific frame still on screen for as long as is desired. A device used quite frequently at the close of a commercial.

Frequency. The number of times an advertising message is delivered within a set period of time.

Frequency discount. A reduction in advertising rates based on the number of insertions in a given period of time.

Full color. See *four color.*

Full position. The preferred position in a newspaper, next to editorial matter or at the top of a column of ads.

Galley. A metal tray on which type is assembled and proofed

Galley proof. A long sheet of paper on which proof of type in galley tray is taken for making corrections.

General advertising. National or nonlocal advertising.

Gimmick. An unusual device or idea used to get attention.

Glossy print. A photograph with smooth surface. It usually gives better reproduction than matte-finish print.

Golden rectangle. A classic shape with a width-depth ratio of 3:5 (or 5:3). Particularly pleasing to the eye.

Gravure. A printing process using ink in the depressions in the plate. When used with a rotary press, it is called *rotogravure*.

Grip. Film-crew members who do various odd jobs on the set, such as lifting and carrying props.

Gross rate. The maximum rate charged by a medium. Includes commissions. See *net rate*.

Gross rating point (GRP). Advertising exposures equal to 1 percent of the population of a market.

Gross rating point buy. The basic outdoor method of sale. A 100-GRP buy is the number of poster panels required to deliver exposure opportunities equal to 100 percent of the population in one day. A 50-GRP buy yields half the exposure opportunities, and so forth.

Gutter. The two inside margins of facing pages.

Hairline. A thin rule or line used for borders and boxes.

Halftone. The process of breaking blacks into small dots and thereby giving a semblance of shades between black and white. Uses screens.

Hand composition. Hand-set type (in contrast to machine set).

Hand lettering. Lettering done by hand, rather than set in type.

Headline. Also *head*. Larger type lines used to get attention in an ad. Usually at top of ad. See *subhead*.

Hidden offer. A special offer buried in copy to test readership.

Hi-fi. Preprinted color ads on better paper than newsprint, with wallpaper design since cut cannot be controlled exactly.

Hitchhike. A short commercial at the end of a program that advertises another product of the sponsor.

Hold. An instruction to typographer to keep type for future use.

Hot type. Type made from metal. See *cold type*.

ID. Short for identification. Usually refers to a 10-second commercial (ordinarily priced at 50 percent to 60 percent of minute rate). Also may refer to a station's on-air promo for itself.

Illustration. Usually a drawing or a painting.

Image. A kind of radio campaign conducted by many stores to enhance the idea customers have of them or to sell customers on shopping there.

Imprint. A small identification sign placed on the molding or skirt of an outdoor structure, stating name of the outdoor company that owns it.

Independent. A station not affiliated with a network.

Information format. A radio format featuring special reports and material, news, interviews.

In-home audience. Radio listeners in the home, as opposed to cars, offices, outdoors.

Insert. Anything printed ahead by an advertiser and sent to the publisher to put into a publication.

Insertion order. Written authorization by an advertiser or ad agency to publish an ad in a specific issue or issues.

Inside panel. Any panel in a group of angled panels, except the one nearest to the line of traffic.

Institute of Outoor Adverising (IOA). The promotion and marketing arm of the outdoor industry.

Institutional advertising. See *corporate advertising*.

Intaglio. Same as *gravure*.

Interlock. The mechanical linkage of separate picture and sound-on-film elements.

Jingle. A musical signature used by advertisers or radio stations to identify themselves to listeners. Jingles vary from complete songs that tell the story to a brief (but memorable) musical intro with an open middle for live or taped copy and perhaps a short musical close. Jingles are frequently prepared in a variety of lengths and seasonal variations for maximum flexibility.

Job press. A printing press for small and short-run jobs.

Job ticket. Written instructions that accompany a printing job through all departments. May be card or envelope.

Justify. In typography, to align the body type so there are even margins on the left and right. All lines are the same length.

Keep standing. Instructions to printer to hold type forms for future use.

Keying copy. Putting a letter (circled) on each copy block on the layout to indicate where copy typed on the copy sheet is to be placed.

Kilohertz. The AM radio frequency: 1,000 cycles a second; the number defining a station's location on AM radio dial, 540 to 1600.

Lap dissolve. A technique employed when one picture disappears as another takes its place.

Lay out. To put the elements of an ad in a pleasing and readable arrangement in a given amount of space. *Layout* is the noun form, the resulting physical "blueprint."

Lead. (pronounced ledd). Extra space between lines of type.

Leaders. A series of dots used to guide the reader's eye.

Letterpress. A method of printing with ink on a raised surface.

Letterspacing. Concerning spacing between letters.

Linage. The amount of ad space expressed in agate lines.

Line plate. Engraving made without screen; only solid blacks.

Linotype. A brand of machine that sets and casts type one line at a time. Another brand is *Intertype*. Creates hot type.

List price. Manufacturer's recommended retail price.

Lithography. Process of printing from a flat surface on which ink is retained by greasy deposit. If transferred to a rubber blanket before printing, the process is called *offset lithography*.

Live copy. The copy read by an announcer in contrast to taped commercials.

Live tag. A message added by the announcer to recorded commercial giving local address, local price, etc. Often used when a manufacturer's radio commercials are aired by store locally.

Local advertising. Advertising placed by a local advertiser, in contrast to national advertising. Also *retail advertising*.

Location. Where the commercial is shot when it is not being photographed in a studio.

Lockup. Type and plates fastened in form for printing, matting, or plating.

Loewy panel. A poster panel designed by Raymond Loewy, featuring light-grey molding of metal or plastic.

Log. A station record of the times commercials and programs were aired as required by FCC.

Logo. A musical or sound effect signature used by an advertiser to identify itself quickly.

Logotype (logo). The name of the advertiser in art or type form that remains the same from ad to ad. See *signature*.

Loss leader. A product offered at cost or below to build store traffic.

Lowercase. Abbreviated l.c. Small letters instead of caps.

LS. Stands for long shot, giving a full view of the set or background.

Ludlow. A brand of machine that casts lines of display-size letters from individual matrices assembled by hand.

Machine composition. Type set by machine, instead of by hand.

Make good. An ad or spot run free by medium to compensate for serious error (i.e., wrong address). Ad costs may be refunded instead.

Makeup. An arrangement of type and plates in page form.

Markdown. A reduction below the original price of the product.

Market. May refer to (1) prospects or (2) a geographical area.

Marketing. The entire system of business activities used to plan, price, promote, and distribute products and services to prospects.

Advertising is only one factor in the marketing process.

Market profile. A description of prospects in terms of demographic, psychographic, and geographic characteristics.

Market segmentation. Dividing the market into homogeneous subsections in order to treat each more appropriately.

Market share. A firm's portion of the industry's total sales.

Markup. The difference between the cost and the selling price of a product.

Mat service. A commercial organization that supplies stock art to advertisers, publications, and printers in the form of mats (cardboard molds) or slicks (for offset publications). See *clip art*.

Medium. A means of communicating: newspapers, magazines, television, radio, direct mail, outdoor, etc. Plural: *media*.

Medium shot. A camera shot that is between a CU and a LS.

Megahertz. One million cycles per second; number defining a station's location on FM radio dial from 88 to 108.

Merchandising. Any activity designed to stimulate trade interest in moving a product or service to the prospect.

Middle-of-the-road (MOR) format. A radio format featuring middle-of-the-road or pop music. Often provides news, information, and sports as well.

Milline rate. A theoretical unit for comparison of newspaper ad rates in relation to circulation.

Minutes. 60-second commercials.

Mix. The rerecording of several audio elements into a single soundtrack.

Molding. The frame of wood or metal that surrounds the face of a bulletin or poster panel.

Monitor. A record of a station's programing and commercials to find out what was aired.

Monotype. A typesetting machine that casts individual letters.

Morning man. The on-air personality hosting the 5–10 A.M. segment of the radio day.

Montage. A number of shots seen in quick succession, sometimes blended into one another.

Mortise. An area cut out of a printing plate to make room for another element.

National advertising. Advertising sponsored by manufacturers who say in their ads: "Buy my brand anywhere." See *retail advertising*.

National Outdoor Advertising Bureau (NOAB). The organization owned and used by advertising agencies for servicing outdoor campaigns.

Net rate. A medium's published rate less agency commission.

Network. A program service supplying news and other programs to affiliates. Four best-known national wired networks are American Broadcasting Co., Columbia Broadcasting System, Mutual Broadcasting System, and National Broadcasting Co.

News format. A radio format featuring continuous news programing.

News hole. Nonadvertising space in a newspaper.

Newsprint. The low-quality paper on which newspapers are printed.

Next-to-reading-matter. Ad position adjacent to editorial content. Supposed to give an ad greater readership.

Off-camera. When the announcer's voice is heard, but he is not seen on the screen. Sometimes referred to as a *voice-over*.

Offset. A lithography printing process using a rubber blanket.

Oldies format. A radio format playing hits of the past, sometimes combined with current hits.

On-camera. When the announcer (or actor) performs in front of the camera.

One-time rate. The rate paid by an advertiser who uses little space (not enough to earn a volume discount). Also *transient rate*.

Open-end. A recorded commercial that provides room at the end for the retailer's "tag."

Open rate. An ad rate for infrequent advertisers, subject to discounts for volume or frequency.

Optical. A term for dissolves, wipes, superimpositions, and other special photographic effects.

Out-of-home audience. Listeners to auto and battery-operated radios outside of the home.

Out of register. Printing in which one impression is not exactly in the spot desired. May give blurry effect.

Outdoor Advertising Association of America (OAAA). The trade association handling research, government regulations, plant service, display standards and public policy for the outdoor industry.

Outline halftone. A halftone in which the background is removed. Also *silhouette*.

Overlay. A transparent flap over art used for giving further instructions, such as color separation, etc. In outdoor, a paper strip providing additional information, such as dealer's name or a sale price, which is pasted on the face of a poster. (See *snipe*.)

Overnight. The time slot from midnight to 5 A.M.

Overrun. A number in excess of specified quantity of copies printed.

Package plan. A combination of spots offered by stations at a discount for fulfilling weekly, monthly, or volume commitments.

Page proof. A proof of type and plates in final page form.

Painted bulletin. An outdoor structure on which copy is painted rather than posted, usually measuring 14' by 48' and sold individually.

Pan. Camera movement in a horizontal direction, left or right, without moving the dolly, or base.

Parallel. An outdoor structure is "parallel" when both ends are within six feet of a line parallel to the line of travel.

Pass-along reader. A person who reads a publication he has not purchased. Readership is greater than circulation.

Pasteup. A layout in which all type and illustrative material are combined for reproduction as a single unit. See *camera-ready*.

Personality. A radio performer who projects enthusiasm, believability and reliability to the radio audience, persuading them to listen to the radio show and buy the products and services advertised.

Photocomposition. Cold type. Type composition by photography.

Photoengraving. A cut or plate made for letterpress printing.

Photostat (stat). A photographic copy. See *PMT* and *Velox*.

Pica. A unit of horizontal type measurement. Six picas equal one inch.

Pick-up. The location from which a program is broadcast. Could be remote from store, sports show from stadium, or news event from another station.

Planographic. Lithography, whether direct or offset.

Plant. All outdoor structures in a given area operated by one company.

Plant capacity. The number of structures operated by an outdoor advertising company.

Plate. A piece of metal from which printing is done. Also *cut*.

PMT. A photostat produced without a negative (like Polaroid process). Faster than *Velox*. Screened print.

Point. A unit of vertical measurement of type: 12 points to a pica; 72 points to an inch.

Poster panel. An outdoor structure minus the advertising message. Most panels measure 12'3" by 24'6" and accommodate both 24-sheet and 30-sheet posters.

Poster—24-Sheet. A poster providing a copy area measuring 8'8" by 19'6".

Poster—30-Sheet. A poster with a copy area of 9'7" by 21'7".

Posting date. The date on which a plant begins to display an advertiser's posters.

Posting period. The length of time during which one poster design is displayed—usually 30 days.

Pounce pattern. A method of projection and tracing used for enlarging art and copy to full painted bulletin size.

Power. Energy measured in watts radiated from a particular station to transmit its programing to listeners' radio sets. Stations' power is specified by the FCC.

Preempt. To replace a regular program or commercial with something of greater interest or more timeliness—often news, political events, or sports broadcasts.

Preferred position. An ad position for which the advertiser pays extra (premium). A specially desirable place (covers).

Premium rate. An extra charge for an especially valuable time-fixed position, news, special events, time, etc.

Preprint. Anything printed prior to publication.

Press proof. A proof made on press before the actual press run.

Press run. The printing of a specific job. Also, the number of copies printed.

Primary colors. In printing: red, yellow, and blue.

Primetime. That period of time in the evening when a station's audience is greatest: 7 P.M. to 11 P.M. in the East and 6 P.M. to 10 P.M. in the Midwest and West.

Printed bulletin. The printed copy posted on a painted bulletin structure.

Producer. An advertising agency coordinator charged with production responsibilities.

Program. A feature of any length (sponsored or unsponsored) aired by a station.

Props. Can refer to the film crew members who handle photographic properties, or to the properties themselves, which may include everything from furniture to ashtrays.

Psychographics. Refers to describing prospects according to their personality and lifestyle traits. See *demographics.*

Publisher's representative (rep). An independent individual or organization that sells advertising space for a publication, usually to national advertisers.

Publisher's statement. A statement of circulation and other information by a publisher.

Pulse. A radio rating service that surveys audiences by personal, in-home interviews.

Ragged. Type set so left or right margins are not aligned or even. Ragged left margins are more difficult to read.

Rate card. A card, folder, or booklet listing various rates and other publishing information for a publication.

Rate holder. A spot run to preserve the conditions of a station contract. Example, being on each week of the year.

Rates. A station's charges for commercial time.

Rating service. A company using sampling methods to survey a population within a defined geographic area to determine the radio listening audience.

Reach. The number of unduplicated people exposed to an advertising message.

Readership. The total audience of a publication, in contrast to the smaller circulation figure. Individuals rather than households.

Reading notice. An ad with the look of an article. No display type.

Register. A condition in which multiple-run printing is done exactly where it is supposed to be.

Reel-to-reel. A tape recorder that records and plays back ¼" magnetic tape at speeds from 1⅞ to 15 ips. Also the tape for this recorder.

Register marks. Cross hairs to aid in securing the right register.

Release. A signed statement by a person giving authorization to use a quote or photograph involving him or her.

Release print. The final print for a TV broadcast.

Relief printing. Raised surface. Letterpress.

Remote. A broadcast from a place other than the station's studio. Remotes may originate at stores for openings and special events.

Renewal. The extension of an existing contract with a station on or before its expiration date.

Representative or rep. Organizations based in major cities whose function is to provide convenient means for a national advertiser to place time locally. Locally, a rep is a term often used for the publisher's or station's salesperson assigned to your account.

Repro proof. A reproduction proof. Clean, sharp proof made from galley ready for paste-up so it can be photographed.

Retail advertising. Also local advertising. Advertising done by retailer who says in his ads, "Buy anything at *my store.*"

Retail trading zone. An area lying outside the city zone. Its residents shop in the city zone to a large degree.

Retouching. Correcting or improving photographs or other art work by using art techniques. Getting ready for making plates.

Reverse. Usually white letters on black, gray, or color background. In body copy, usually discouraged as harder to read.

Riding the showing. A physical inspection of the panels that comprise a showing.

Rights. Charges to a station for the right to broadcast a sporting event. If the event is sponsored, the sponsor pays the bill.

Rock format. Refers to stations featuring rock music, usually emphasizing most popular current hits.

Rotary press. In letterpress, a press that prints from curved plates on cylinders, rather than on a flat bed.

Rotation. Repeating a series of ads in the order in which they appeared.

Rotogravure. Gravure printing on a rotary press. See *gravure.*

Rough. A preliminary sketch showing where type and art are to go.

Rough cut. The first attempt at editing the commercial picture.

Rule. A thin line used for borders or boxes in ads.

Run-of-paper (ROP). The position of your ad in the newspaper will be up to the paper itself. Usually, it is better to request a general section (sports, women's, etc.).

Run of schedule (ROS). Same as BTA.

SAG. The Screen Actor's Guild. The performers' union covering film talent who work for established scales of pay.

Sans serif. In typography, a type that has no cross strokes or serifs at the tops and bottoms of characters.

Saturation. A heavy schedule of commercials that gets the message across to as many listeners as possible. A popular use of saturation is for events and sales.

Scaling. Reducing or enlarging an illustration or photo.

Schedule. The times of day and/or dates an advertiser's commercials or ads run in a specific campaign or continuing program, with timings, sizes, etc.

Scripts. Radio copy. Also called continuity.

Segue. Fading one audio element into another.

Separation. Commercial protection. The station provides a set time period between competitors.

Serifs. The short cross strokes at top and bottom of characters in certain typefaces, especially those in Roman face.

Set solid. Lines of type without leading (or space) between.

Setback. The distance measured from the line of travel to the center of the poster panel or painted bulletin.

Sheet-fed press. A press that takes individual sheets of paper rather than rolls of paper.

Short rate. If an advertiser fails to use the amount of space contracted for, he is charged the higher rate he did earn.

Share of audience. The percentage of tuned-in audience listening to each station at any given time.

Short rate. The charge back to the advertiser for not fulfilling his contract.

Showing. A unit of poster sales that is an alternative to Gross Rating Points. Showings are designated as #100, #75, #50, #25. There is often a close correlation between a showing number and a GRP number.

Sign-off. The time at which a station goes off-air daily.

Sign-on. The time at which a station goes on-air daily.

Signature. The advertiser's name in an ad. Abbreviated *sig*.

Silhouette. Art subject with background removed.

Silk screen. A method of printing based on the stencil principle. Ink is squeezed through a silk screen.

Single rate card. A station rate card in which the same rates apply to national and local advertisers.

Sixties. 60-second or minute commercials.

Slug. A line of type produced by a linecasting machine.

Small caps. Capital letters smaller than regular capital letters in that type size.

Sneak. When music is brought in at low volume. Thus, to "sneak in" means to bring music in without distracting the listeners.

Snipe. An additional message pasted over a poster to identify dealers or give price or other information. (See *overlay*.)

Space position value. An index of the visibility of poster panel based on length of approach, speed of traffic, angle of the panel, and its relationships to nearby panels.

Spanish format. A radio format featuring Hispanic-oriented music with community news.

Spectacolor. Preprinted page ads on rolls, like hi-fi, but with attachment on press to control where cut is to be made.

Sponsor. An advertiser who buys a radio program.

Spot. A commercial or announcement.

Spot radio. Also called national spot. A national radio buy that allows an advertiser to buy commercials in many markets by buying individual stations as needed to meet marketing objectives.

Spotted map. A town, city, or market map marked to show the placement of panels or painted bulletins.

Spread. Two facing pages in a publication, used as single ad.

Standard colors. Bulletin colors adopted by the OAAA and paint manufacturers as standard for outdoor advertising.

Standard of paper. The sheets of paper making up one complete poster.

Standing ad. An ad that is run unchanged for a long period of time.

Stat. A photographic print. Velox or PMT are two types. *Photostat.*

Stereotype. A duplicate plate cast from mat.

Stet. A proofreading term meaning leave as was; ignore change.

Stock music. Previously recorded music available in a music library.

Stock shot. A piece of film already on file in a film library, which is used instead of original footage.

Storyboard. An artist's rendition of a commercial, usually drawn on paper in separated frames.

Strip. A program or spot purchased at the same time each day.

Strip-in. Combining two or more negatives for production as a single plate.

Subhead. May be (1) a display line enlarging on the main headline, usually in smaller size, or (2) a short heading inside the copy used to break up long patches of gray.

Super. The abbreviation for a superimposition. When pictures, or words, are imposed in front of another picture and both are seen at the same time.

Supplement. A special section—sometimes in tabloid format—distributed in regular newspaper. Usually it has a single theme. Also refers to Sunday magazine sections.

Swipe file. An idea person's library of examples of ads, etc., done by other people. Used for inspiration.

Sync. The abbreviation for synchronization. The exact matching of sound and picture elements.

Tabloid. A newspaper (or section) half the standard size.

Tag. An anouncement at the end of a recorded commercial that supplies additional information.

Talent. A radio performer, either on programs or commercials or both.

Talk format. A radio format that devotes all or most of air time to interviews or audience features. Usually does not program music.

Tape. Verb: record a commercial or other sound for future on-air use. Noun: magnetic tape that sound is recorded on.

Tear sheet. A full page showing the ad as run. Used for checking.

Teaser. An ad designed for curiosity by leaving out the name of the sponsor. Successive ads may add a little more information each time.

Tens. 10-second commercials.

Thirties. 30-second commercials.

Thumbnail. A rough layout in miniature, at the doodling stage.

Till forbid (TF). Instructions to a newspaper to continue running an ad as scheduled until further notice.

Tilt. Camera movement in a vertical direction.

Tilt-up. Camera movement up. (Tilt-down—camera movement down.)

Time classifications. Various time slots during broadcast day priced differently depending on size of audience.

Timer. An automatic switch on illuminated displays to turn lights on and off at predetermined times.

Tint block. A light shade of ink used as a background for type, etc.

Title crawl. A series of titles moves across the screen, appearing at the bottom, disappearing at the top.

Total audience plan (TAP). A spot package providing a set number of spots in each of the station's time classifications. The TAP schedule will reach all of the station's listeners in the specified time period. Other names for this kind of package include impact plan, saturation plan.

Trademark. A word or symbol attached to merchandise or package or placed in an ad to identify the maker or origin.

Trade name. The company name under which a firm does business, i.e., General Motors. Contrasted with brand name (Chevrolet).

Traffic. Departments in ad agencies and at stations responsible for seeing that spots are run at the right times with the designated copy.

Traffic Audit Bureau (TAB). An organization sponsored by outdoor plants, advertising agencies, and advertisers to authenticate outdoor circulation.

Transient rate. A flat or one-time rate, with no discounts.

Trim. The molding and borders of various designs used to frame poster panels and painted bulletins.

Type family. A group of type faces with the same basic design, but with variations in width of characters, boldness, etc.

Type high. The height of letterpress plates and type: .918 inch.

Typo. A typographical error.

Typography. The field involving designing, setting, and using type.

Unit. A single poster panel or painted bulletin.

Unity. A design principle that says all elements of an ad should be related. Done with overlapping elements, connecting lines, background color, etc.

Uppercase (U.C.). Capital letters. Usually called *caps*.

Velox. A photostatic print that has been screened. Less expensive than regular halftone process. Also see PMT.

Vertical saturation. Slotting commercials heavily on several stations before a sale and on the sale day itself to reach the maximum number of customers.

Video. Refers to the picture portion of a TV commercial.

Visualization. The process of mentally picturing how an ad will look, before it is produced. Also, getting an idea into visual or graphic form.

Voice-over. The off-camera voice of an announcer who is heard but not seen.

Waste circulation. Copies of a publication that go to an area where product is not distributed or is so far away people would not come that far to buy.

Web-fed press. A printing press that uses a roll of paper.

White space. The space in an ad not taken with any other element, type, pictures, etc. An important design element in itself.

Whiz pan. An optical device to go quickly from one scene to another, in which the camera is swung rapidly from left to right, or vice-versa.

Widow. Type that is less than a full line, particularly one with only a single word or two. Usually discouraged.

Wipe. An optical device that "wipes" away one picture on screen to reveal another.

Wrong font (WF). A proofreader's mark to tell the typographer that character from one font has been mixed with another.

Zinc. Slang for photoengraving.

Zoned edition. Part of a newspaper's circulation going to a specific geographical area (i.e., suburb). A section of the edition or a page of a section may have editorial matter just for that zone. Advertisers located within that area are allowed to advertise only in copies going to that area, and do not pay for unwanted waste circulation.

Zoom. The slow or rapid movement toward or away from a person or object on the screen. A zoom shot is effected by a special lens on the camera.

About the Authors

Albert C. Book has been chairman of the Advertising Department at the University of Nebraska for twelve years. Awarded the M.B.A. degree by New York University, he has also taught at the University of Iowa, N.Y.U., and the University of Texas at Austin.

Professor Book began his 20-year advertising career as advertising manager for the H.C. Burns Co., Oakland, California, in 1945. Since then, he has served as copywriter and account executive for Al Paul Lefton Advertising; copy chief, Furman Advertising; and copy supervisor, Batten, Barton, Durstine & Osborn, from 1955 to 1963. After assuming his present position as Professor of Journalism, Professor Book continued to work as creative consultant for such advertising firms as Bozell & Jacobs.

In addition to teaching, managing, and copywriting, Professor Book has been a sports writer, book reviewer, and film and drama critic for newspapers in San Francisco and New York. He was also director of the National Collegiate Athletic Association Task Force of the American Broadcasting Company in the mid-1950s.

Professor Book has co-authored a widely used textbook on creating broadcast commercials—*The Radio and Television Commercial*, which is now in its second edition (1984).

C. Dennis Schick has been Executive Director of the Arkansas Press Association since 1979. An active advertising consultant, he conducts numerous seminars and workshops each year and speaks to many and varied groups about advertising.

Dr. Schick has a B.A. in Journalism and English from Texas Christian University, a Master's degree in Advertising and Marketing from the University of Illinois at Champaign-Urbana, and a Ph.D. in Mass Communication and Marketing from Southern Illinois University.

He taught advertising, journalism, and public relations at TCU, SIU, Oklahoma State University, and the University of Texas at Austin before assuming his current position.

In addition, he has worked for weekly and daily newspapers in Texas, Oklahoma, and Illinois, both in advertising sales and management, and as a writer, photographer, and columnist.

Besides co-authoring *Fundamentals of Copy and Layout*, Dr. Schick has written a textbook on newspaper advertising—*How to Create Newspaper Advertising that Moves Merchandise*—and a lab manual on graphics.